SOCIAL CONSTRUCTION
AND NEWS WORK

Social Construction and News Work

Newsworkers, Civic Function, and
Resistance in the Changing Media World

William Schulte

<teneo> //press
AMHERST, NEW YORK

Copyright 2014 Teneo Press

All rights reserved
Printed in the United States of America

No part of this publication may be reproduced, stored in or introduced into a retrieval system, or transmitted, in any form, or by any means (electronic, mechanical, photocopying, recording, or otherwise), without the prior permission of the publisher.

Requests for permission should be directed to:
permissions@teneopress.com, or mailed to:
Teneo Press
PO Box 349
Youngstown, NY 14174

Library of Congress Control Number: xxx

Schulte, William.
The Social Construction and News Work: Newsworkers, Civic Function, and Resistance in the Changing Media World.
p. cm.
Includes bibliographical references and index.
ISBN 978-1-934844-68-7 (alk. paper).

For Jackie, Harper, and Ila, of course.

Table of Contents

Acknowledgments ix
Chapter 1: Reflecting Newsworkers 1
Chapter 2: Influence Within and Beyond 11
Chapter 3: The Process of Newspaper News Work 35
Chapter 4: How Newsworkers See Their World 49
Chapter 5: Modern Social Controls 67
Chapter 6: Autonomy and Resistance 101
Chapter 7: Conclusion 119
Appendix 135
References 145
Index 153

Acknowledgments

It is with respect that I thank my classmates and mentors at Ohio University for guiding me to the construction of this book. Never have I learned so much or found so much gratification as I have at the Scripps School of Journalism. I must give special thanks to Marilyn Greenwald, my dissertation chair, for her encouragement and belief in this project. I also thank the members of my dissertation committee: Joseph Bernt, whose practical knowledge of academia made my road smooth; Duncan Brown, who taught me theory, law, and how to be a better teacher; and Gene Ammarell, my anthropology mentor, who taught me government, economics, and that organizations should promote human dignity. I also owe thanks to many other amazing professors who brought me to this point. To name a few: Carson B Wagner, Hong Chang, Patrick Washburn, Mark H. Massé, and Mark Popovich.

I sincerely appreciate my loving family. Foremost, I must thank my loving wife, Jacqueline, a great editor without whom none of this would have been possible. I thank my darling daughters, Harper and Ila Wren, for inspiring me; my mother, Patricia, who passed away before she could see this project come to fruition but whose spirit watched over every step; my father, Edward, who taught me to never, never give up; my sister, Betty, who gave me invaluable feedback; my brother Michael, who taught me that the challenges of life can be conquered through good humor and hard work; and my brother John, who never stopped believing in me.

I also thank the newspapers examined in this study for giving me access to their operations. Lastly, I thank all of the newsworkers I encountered during this study and when I was in the journalism profession. What you do is so important.

Social Construction and News Work

Chapter 1

Reflecting Newsworkers

Looking at news organizations often seems to involve a one-way mirror. The organization can see out into the public to do reporting or to interact with sources, but when the public tries to see in, the glass is black. Newspapers are involved with the public as members of their business communities, and reporters are present at many community events. The communities themselves are not usually privy to newsroom dynamics and often assume that the stereotypes portrayed in entertainment are a reflection of the reality of that world. This is a dangerous assumption considering the role of news organizations as government watchdogs and as the eyes of the public.

Scholars are often guilty of these oversights as well, but in different ways. Many follow the traditions of media history—in terms of power, progress, and capitalism—to inform their understanding of the institution of journalism. Perhaps this is not wrong, but it does leave a hole in the knowledge of media mechanics because following these traditions does not necessarily address the contributions of rank-and-file newsworkers and their direct influences on journalism. The media often constitute a darkened field in the public's eye, and audiences cannot penetrate the influences in that field so as to understand all that comes to bear on their eyes and ears. This is the newsworker's world.

This book represents an effort to understand the roles newsworkers play in many newsrooms and to understand the pressures, influences, realities, and structures these individuals experience in their jobs, as well as their place in the contemporary climate of media capitalism. This is a dynamic and challenging period for newsworkers as competing forces like the Internet and other digital platforms force their organizations to re-create themselves. For many years publishers have scrambled to bring costs into line with thinning revenues. In this effort more than 35,000 newspaper jobs have been eliminated during the last five years. This includes 4,111 newspaper jobs that were jettisoned in 2011 (Smith, n.d.). Those numbers continue to rise; notably, June 2013 saw the layoff of the entire *Chicago Sun-Times* photo staff. Further, digital and online media have all but broken the traditional advertising-supported business model of the American newspaper. This is the model that served media organizations well during the rise of the American press.

This study relates to the commodification of the news but does not follow corporate interests beyond their effects in newsrooms themselves. Newsworkers have an interesting history. They have been caught in the middle of the rise of journalism as mass entertainment, and therefore much of their work has been sensationalized. They have been held responsible both for maintaining the status quo in society and for its unfavorable changes. They have been both the mouthpieces of corporate America and the strongest advocates for freedom of the press. According to Hanno Hardt and Bonnie Brennen (1995),

> Their middle-class backgrounds or ambitions were deflected, despite promises of professionalism, and squashed by the social and economic realities of news work within a social and political climate that fostered industrial growth and led to the triumph of business interests. Their own voices were rarely heard and their story remains to be told. (p. viii)

Reflecting Newsworkers 3

In these pages readers will find the results of a collection of formal interviews and observations made among working journalists who perform jobs in various aspects of news production. *Social Construction and News Work* incorporates the ethnographic tradition of participant observation, the collection of documents, in-depth interviews, and informal conversations. The intention is to give newsworkers a voice while attempting to understand their changing industry. The hope is that doing so will provide insight into how those changes are affecting newsworkers' lives, work, and attitudes. It is also a goal of this study to contribute to a literature base that sees the contributions of newsworkers as critical to understanding media reality, for it is a unique culture, environment, and site of struggle regarding the conditions of industry and civic function. This study is an ethnography of several newsrooms written to enhance the understanding of the newsworker's world and to help define what progress has been made in terms of education, experience, community knowledge, and service in the realm of newspaper journalism. These are the areas of human capital that give newsworkers a meaningful and dignified experience in what was once decidedly a patron-client relationship with their employers.

The history of the newsworker parallels the history of American labor. Industrial growth, labor relations, education, and craft skills in the service of entrepreneurship—and later of large corporate interests—lie at the heart of their work, and newsworkers at all levels have been instrumental in laying the groundwork for what is valued in the profession today.

This book is not a comprehensive examination of all those who serve among news work's rank and file, although press workers, circulation staff, clerical workers, and distribution specialists are certainly important players in any news operation and are worthy of attention. This study is about the journalism professionals who gather, report, and present news and information for the benefit of the public. Moreover, it is about those professionals who do this in news organizations that produce a print product as part of their daily mission. This is not to imply that the only newsworkers worthy of the name exist in a newspaper environment. Broadcasters at every level, community bloggers, and backpack journalists are also key players, but this work is intended as a deep look inside a specific part of a much wider industry. This study is also not indicative of all the manifestations of print journalism but rather is a reflection of the newspapers and newsworkers observed for this study that might be characterized as common manifestations in the industry. The findings herein preserve the anonymity of both informants and organizations. This condition certainly promotes honesty, but it also gives this work a false sense of universality and generality that should be noted from the start. Broadly accepted dynamics are certainly reflected in the work, but this book is intended as a canary in a coal mine to reveal trends and issues, some organizational dynamics, and the evolving newspaper world.

This study uses *newsworker* as a single word to generally refer to line editors, reporters, designers, copy editors, photographers, digital specialists, and all the variations thereof who contribute to the goals of journalism, work within an organization's for-profit structure, and are not upper-echelon management. Peter Berger and Thomas Luckmann's (1966) definition of the *social construction of reality* guides this study, for it explains how reality is formed by social systems over time. Social constructionism in the newsroom, as elsewhere, is the representation of individual actions habituated into roles played by those in a workplace in relation to their institutional identity. When these roles play out, the reciprocal interactions are institutionalized. In the process of this institutionalization, meaning becomes embedded in the culture of a newsroom, and belief about what reality is becomes embedded in the institutional fabric of the group. This is what is meant by *social constructionism*. A range of literature related to the social construction of reality and the individual level of news work is explored in this book to help situate this study among others of similar purpose and to inform the reader.

Reflecting Newsworkers 5

This book suggests that newsworkers are fundamentally influential in the development of public communication and that their influence, though challenged, is profound, even under the shadow of corporate media ownership, changing technology, and downsizing. This study takes a snapshot of workers who shape contemporary media; adding to the understanding of the traditions of labor and the Fourth Estate will help scholars categorize the utility and intention of this work.

Many media studies concentrate on influences, which are much more macro focused than an examination of the individual newsworker is; other media research focuses on the effects of content. These studies are certainly important for protecting the interests of media users but add little to an understanding of the production process or of the reasons news content takes the forms that it does. This approach has generated a top-down way of looking at the American press that privileges property and ownership at the expense of a deep understanding of news work (Hardt & Brennen, 1995).

This study addresses the need to chronicle newsworkers as the industry struggles to morph into something viable in the modern age and adds to the literature that has chronicled this shift from the beginning of newspaper history. An old adage among newsworkers is that journalism is a first draft of history, but the history of newsworkers themselves has only just started to catch up with other industry chronicles. The result of this study is a journey through the ways newsworkers do their jobs, the understanding newsworkers have of their industry, and the ongoing challenges they face as journalists. In the following chapters, economic forces and social construction find their way into the narrative, but the newsworkers' attitudes and voices take center stage.

In this research, I examine the history of newsworkers in terms of social construction research, technology, and the individual newsworker's influence as these factors merge into a single cultural dynamic. Social control has often been approached as a phenomenon beyond individuals' influence, but an alternate reading of the literature finds that it is also a collective dynamic in which individual influence plays an active role in constructing reality. I examine the social construction model, news work, organizational influences, and policy so as to understand the reality beyond that which is socially constructed in the newsroom and to inform the newsworker dynamics observed in subsequent chapters. In order to do this, I have identified issues from the past that are still important to newsworkers, such as the ways the modern newsroom engages civic function, traditional routines, morale, influence, professionalism, and digital technologies. Chapter 2 records a search for consistent patterns in the exploration of the social world of newsworkers and seeks evidence of newsworkers' exploring or not exploring that question for themselves.

Chapter 3 looks at the process of news work, takes the reader through the structures of a typical newsroom, and explores the various tasks and routines required to produce a newspaper or a related media product on deadline. This chapter explores the naturalized processes that have been the tradition of news work for a very long time and observes how these tasks have changed to make room for new technology and to allow a slimmer work force. The chapter also examines digital and technological considerations and tasks that have added to the complexity of the work. I define for this book such different newsroom positions as news gatherers, presenters, and digital specialists and reveal their unique contributions and their daily pressures. From this foundation, understandings of modern organizational controls become apparent and are evaluated in terms of Warren Breed's (1955) social controls. The chapter sees the newsworker's world as more convoluted than it was in the past, for it now involves added policies, evolving technology, and administrators who are unable to focus on daily routines. This is a world ripe for mistakes, lawsuits, and a mass exodus of overwhelmed personnel.

Chapter 4 is guided by in-depth interviews with newsworkers and is intended to provide a starting point for the later participant-observation phase of the project. The goal was to determine the concerns of newsworkers and how they have viewed the challenges inherent in their jobs throughout their careers. Many journalists have grown fearful of losing their livelihoods as the industry has seen extreme and unprecedented layoffs in the last few years. Many do not feel appreciated for the traditional journalism skills they practice. Some newsworkers are excited about the paradigm shift from print to digital journalism, but still more are threatened not only by the technology but also by younger newsworkers who are adept at digital journalism and less expensive to employ. The social controls of the newsroom identified by Warren Breed in 1955 are still very much part of newsroom culture, but these controls have evolved to be more explicit and overtly enforced by management. The economic priorities of executives that take precedence over journalistic ideas are transparent to newsworkers, even as management poorly communicates what an organization needs if it is to remain viable. Newsworkers harbor a profound distrust of their employing organizations. This distrust is so strong that many newsworkers feel they are being actively plotted against, a situation that fosters cautious journalism and low job satisfaction. In the face of these challenges, newsworkers reveal passion for the civic duty of the press and diverse interests outside the workplace.

Chapter 5 updates the classic social controls of the newsroom first explored by Warren Breed and adds to those controls by identifying several new policies and priorities at work in the modern dynamic. Authority and sanctions have become much more overt as organizations have struggled with knowing what is needed from newsworkers in today's difficult financial and technological terrain. At the same time, newsworkers find it difficult to advance in organizations or move to other news jobs as operations downsize. Many newsworkers do not respect their superiors, as was once the norm in the industry, and their interactions with administrators can be decidedly adversarial. Administrators have been directed to favor digital over traditional skills. Technology has demystified many once-sacred newsroom tasks, such as photography and the publishing process itself. The result is a loss of respect for rank-and-file workers, layoffs, conspiracies to implement layoffs, and the amalgamation of positions. Newsworkers are often blindsided by changes as executives plot reallocation of resources and personnel above a "black ceiling" beyond which newsworkers cannot see. As a result, newsworkers are often apprehensive about interactions with superiors and are unsure about the perceived quality of their job performance.

Chapter 6 focuses on the ways newsworkers resist as organizations introduce directive after directive challenging their core principles. Newsworkers often have forceful personalities and have developed clever ways to use the tides that are shifting toward digital media to control their workloads and create favorable opportunities for themselves. Executives, like newsworkers, are struggling to understand new technology, and because the information-delivery platforms are changing quickly, they do not have the focus to monitor all newsworker activity. In addition, some newsworkers have found ways to send messages of dissatisfaction to their employers by not supporting goals outside the direct practices of their work. This resistance takes the form of not giving time or money to charity fundraisers and not volunteering for promotional endeavors. Such relationships as interoffice marriages create buffers for criticism by bolstering support between spheres of influence and discouraging criticism within those spheres. "Sunshine blogs" keep newsworkers connected to decision making above the black ceiling, and these blogs fill a void in fellowship that has been lost through the demise or marginalization of many unions. Resisting organizational directives has become as naturalized a process as issuing the directives themselves. Newsworkers have found ways to work around them through apathy, citing precedent, and manipulating their daily routines —or simply by the force of their personalities.

Chapter 7 synthesizes what has been learned about influence. Newsworkers cannot be separated in any sustainable way from the civic responsibility of journalism or from the traditional crafts associated with its practice. The labor of journalism is as much a spiritual endeavor for its practitioners as it is a profession. At the same time, organizations fail to see—or at least fail to acknowledge—that removing the civic aspects of the newsworkers' world results in the removal of passion, loyalty, and respect. Digital endeavors are not valued with the same reverence the printed newspaper is accorded by newsworkers at any rank-and-file level beyond the digital experts themselves. This is because the Internet and digital platforms lack physical permanence and because of their short history in relation to that of many newsworkers; many newsworkers do not approach such media with the same sense of seriousness they allow print. These areas form points of great friction between executives and newsworkers, and both sides have exploited these dynamics in newsrooms.

CHAPTER 2

INFLUENCE WITHIN AND BEYOND

Research about professional dynamics has mostly concentrated on three key areas: the identity of journalism as a profession and its relevance in a networked society, the self-reflection of journalists about possible changes to their professional identities, and the challenges posed by user-authored content to the jurisdictional space that newsworkers occupy as gatekeepers of information (Mitchelstein & Boczkowski 2008). The public largely expects that the individuals who collect, produce, and present news are the most influential players in constructing those images as a reflection of reality. But the dominant literature on the pressures and influences on the American newsworker over the years has indicated that this simply is not the case. According to Gaye Tuchman (1972), each story a newsworker produces has the potential to affect his or her professional mobility, and that individual's daily actions affected the ability of the organization to make a profit. In the newsroom of old, the landscape was dangerous for even the most stalwart newsworkers. They needed to make quick decisions that influenced validity, reliability, and truth on a daily basis. This has only been exacerbated in the digital age, and context is often lost. Alain de Botton (2014) called this the institutional amnesia of the news hub. "The pace of the news cycle is relentless. However momentous yesterday's news—the landslides, the discovery of a young girl's half-concealed body, the humiliation of once-powerful politicians—every morning the cacophony begins afresh" (p. 252).

Traditional pressures have blended with multimedia and other tasks in a phenomenon Michael Bromley (1997) called *multiskilling*. However, multiskilling does not necessitate mastering different newsroom tasks. Eric Klinenberg (2005) examined several news operations in the United States and found that the pressures associated with additional tasks and the requirement to post up-to-the-minute news compromised their proficiency.

Online news production is certainly a continuing influence in the modern newsroom; however, traditions like information gathering and a distrust of the Internet as a source of information persist. Eugenia Mitchelstein and Pablo J. Boczkowski (2008) have suggested that many professionals and audiences embrace the novelty and opportunity represented in an online platform. They concluded that news production exists between tradition and change.

The concept of a social construction of reality as explored by Peter Berger and Thomas Luckmann (1966) reveals that such social organizations as newsrooms over time form a mental picture of the roles played by individuals as they relate to one another. This social construction informs the way individuals interact, and behaviors start to perpetuate until this construction is institutionalized as the norm. In other words, belief in what reality is becomes reality. These viewpoints reflect what may be called a constructionist paradigm, which asserts that for a dynamic to be understood one must examine the artifacts of the culture (Johnson-Cartee, 2005). This concept takes on great complexity as one considers the abstract values ingrained in news work—values that include but are not limited to ethics, civic responsibility, and objectivity. There are also less-heralded views that all newsworkers bring to their work, such as world view, education, and home life. As individuals engage and interact in the various aspects of life, they develop certain dispositions toward their identities and the ways they are expected to behave. Through these dispositions, combined with other complex social behaviors and expectations, many will start to understand their place in the social order and begin to embody this expectation in their habitus.

These complex traits are incorporated into the context of a capitalist endeavor, the working newsroom. Social constructionist theory dictates that the collective defines the individual. To say, however, that an individual newsworker's influence is challenged is not to say that it is nonexistent. In fact, the influence of newsworkers—considered in terms of social constructionist thought—is extremely powerful. Berger and Luckmann also found that although reality is socially constructed, concrete individuals serve as the agents of that reality. This makes the motivations of those definers—in this case, newsworkers—paramount.

When evaluating the newsroom community using an approach informed by a socially constructed reality, one should consider the ways newsworkers have been disenfranchised by the dominant theoretical paradigm in this area. After all, there are many voices at work in the construction of reality.

The hierarchy of influence model proposed by Pamela Shoemaker and Stephen Reese (1996) also has some utility in understanding influence; it sees the newsworker's level of influence squeezed by routines, organizational controls, extramedia concerns, and ideology. In this model, the levels of influence explain the hierarchical structure of organizations and outside influences. The individual is at the center of this model, and the individual's level of influence is reflected through the education and professionalism of each journalist. The next-higher levels of influence are media routines (journalistic practices), the organization (organizational goals, roles, structures, and controls), extramedia concerns (social issues, economic concerns, and economic climate), and ideology (the political and economic systems under which they operate). The overall effect of this hierarchy is that individual newsworkers appear constrained under the weight of forces beyond their control.

Nonetheless, the ability of a newsworker to direct content has been explored in the past and never wholly abandoned. David Manning White (1955) and Pamela Shoemaker (1999) illustrated the newsworker's control in the news process by exploring the concept of gatekeeping, the premise that before it reaches the public, information passes through a series of gates in the form of newsroom decision making. These gates are the newsworkers' independent hand of authority over the information that reaches the public. This idea has met with resistance among many modern scholars. The dominant wisdom is that gatekeeping oversimplifies a complex process and neglects to explain the pressures put on newsworkers while they do their jobs.

Warren Breed (1955) found that newsworkers had been disenfranchised by a series of social controls, often in the form of sanctions, put in place by executives and publishers. He wrote, "[A]ny important change toward a more free and responsible press must stem from various possible pressures on the publisher, who epitomizes the policy-making and coordinating role" (Breed, p. 84). Tuchman (1978), in her look at strategic ritual, reiterated that reporters must protect themselves from dominating influences. She identified an obsessive observation of objectivity as a means of distancing reporters, keeping them from exerting their influence. Much of the literature concerning social control has supported this position. However, much of the literature concerning the social construction of reality and of media has focused on how this social construction has affected the consumers of media rather than on how it affects the newsworkers themselves.

Much past work focused on social construction can be applied to the internal workings of news gatherers by taking a fresh look at some of the texts. To do so, this book turns the mirror back onto newsworkers and news organizations in order to better understand influence, resistance, and reality in the modern newsroom. Pamela Shoemaker and Stephen

Reese found that "the individual level of influence is useful in determining what the communicator thinks is worth transmitting to his or her audience and how the story should be developed ... [although] organizationally defined factors have direct impact on mass media content" (p. 103).

It is uncertain how Shoemaker and Reese intended this individual level of influence to be received in their model, but rather than viewing the influence model as having overpowering elements that force the individual level of influence into a position trapped by the other levels, one can make the case that the individual level is at the core of the model for a reason, both figuratively and literally. A close examination of newsroom culture's influences on news work beyond the individual makes a good starting point for understanding the systems under which they operate. Thus, in this chapter I first explore the newsroom culture as a collective dynamic operating in parallel with these other hierarchical considerations and then examine how individual realities have been explored in the past. Collectively, these considerations position the study for its examination of the modern newsroom.

UNDERSTANDING SOCIAL CONSTRUCTION BEYOND THE INDIVIDUAL

Social control as it has been used to examine pressures in news work and influences beyond the individual level has been explored in many ways. Many scholars assert that digital transition has obscured what a journalist truly is (Allan, 2006; Kopper, Kolthoff, & Czepek, 2000; Singer, 2003).

Ben Bagdikian (1990) offered some insight into the organizational and extramedia level of influence when he, along with many others, claimed that media's pursuit of advertising dollars made them structurally dependent on business, and that such dependence has restricted news content. Philip Schlesinger (1978) found routines to be more than just a way to meet deadlines and manage a complex world for audiences. He noted that the routines of news programs are affected by political, economic, and ideological constraints that make news production akin to propaganda. Schlesinger found that newsworkers on the front line of production could make only cosmetic changes that appeared profound to other professionals because of their novelty.

Edward Herman and Noam Chomsky (1988) found a model of propaganda more explanatory of organizational control. They utilized the conventions of political economy to explore the influences that affected news production and suggested that capitalist forces and the bourgeoisie were interlocked with media ownership and reflected the dominant ideology of the states in which they were found. This placed newsworkers in the Marxist position of a proletariat. In this line of thinking, journalism supports a superstructure that favors those who control the means of production, and where individuals find themselves in terms of that means of production determines how their reality is constructed. As Karl Marx and Friedrich Engels (1848/1998) wrote in *The Communist Manifesto*, the ideas of the ruling class are, in every age, the ruling ideas: That is, the class that is the dominant material force in society is at the same time its dominant intellectual force. However, journalism is more than a manufacturing process, and its expert craft has rarely been associated with the American wealthy class (the one percent, so to speak). This makes bourgeoisie influence in the direct decision making of a newsroom questionable. Rather, the social structures and the conventions of journalism are more likely to determine day-to-day influence.

Émile Durkheim (1912/2008) took a mass-society approach to the social world. He observed that the social structures required for creating solidarity in society constitute "social fact." He asserted that in spite of individual ideas and will, groups have social mechanisms in place to create "mechanical solidarity" for the purpose of perpetuating the structure. Social facts are the established, expected, or conventional ways of behaving laid down in custom, law, or precedent. These components of mass society theory are also reflected in Marxist thought in one key way: both remove the individual from a position of self-agency. Owners of large media organizations and their publishers can be seen as among the ruling class, whereas newsworkers generally are not and therefore have often been seen as doing their employers' bidding.

As the values of journalists, their societal positions, and their representative behaviors have perpetuated themselves over the years, Pierre Bourdieu's (1984) ideas about social space (peer networks) and social capital (the nonfinancial social value of an individual) have been at work in newsrooms. Journalism comes with its own set of social facts and mechanical solidarity. Belief in the civic responsibly of the press is only one of many unifying principles in the social world of the journalist. The goal of conveying that civic responsibly to the audience creates mechanical solidarity within the job.

Much of the discourse regarding influence at the ideological or the extramedia level involves consolidated ownership and the ways in which reality comes to be poorly reflected. Ownership across multiple media platforms has led to restrictions in social discourse as news choices are limited (Herman & Chomsky, 1988). "Most biased choices in the media arise from the preselection of right-thinking people, internalized preconceptions, and the adaptation of personnel to the constraints of ownership, organization, market, and political power" (p. xii). The assertion that right-thinking people are a necessary component to influence over coverage implies that the influence of the rank and file is profound.

The idea of the imposing hand of corporate hegemony was taken a step further in Doug Underwood's (1993) study *When MBAs Rule the Newsroom*, which focuses on newspapers as a product versus journalism as a practice. Underwood cited Susan Miller, then the E. W. Scripps Company vice president of news, who reframed a pandering ideology as reflecting a commitment to service and strongly indicated that any editor not on board with this concept would be driven out. This silencing of newsroom voices damaged and alienated newsworkers and limited opportunities for a pluralistic presentation of news. Underwood also noted that this practice has not improved the financial position of most newspapers:

> They [management] are too willing to squeeze news resources and space for news in service to corporate demands and the pressures of Wall Street; they suppress aggressive in-depth reporting for the sake of formula journalism; and they have created a newsroom environment increasingly inhospitable to the independent, irreverent, and challenge-the-world personalities that have traditionally been attracted to the profession of daily newspapering. (Underwood, 1993, p. xiv)

Some have predicted that diversity as it relates to media ownership, trust protection, and voice in media will likely be reassessed in the face of new media's growth. The phenomenon of declining audiences, along with the consolidation of media outlets, is raising concerns about antitrust policy. A refined reading of the First Amendment could be the next step; the Supreme Court has indicated that the rights of the people—not the owners of media—should be paramount (Stucke & Grunes, 2009).

Edward Jay Epstein's (1973) *News from Nowhere* examines the structures behind network news on television—specifically, NBC News, CBS News, and ABC News. Epstein observed the ways in which various methods of selecting and gathering news may affect the final product. According to him, a great deal of research and thought was devoted to propaganda and publicity but little to the news-gathering process itself. He found that the final product reflected a distorted reality. The structures imposed so as to construct events as stories became the values involved in news culture. The personal values of newsworkers were not decisive when in conflict with an organization's values, despite their being an important input into the news process.

The Glasgow University Media Group (1976) asserted that "contrary to the claims, conventions, and culture of television journalism, the news is not a neutral product" (p. 10). The group discovered that the concept of cultural neutrality is false and contended that the mass media are dysfunctional for social change. Rather, they reinforce the power structures of the society in which they operate. News selection is "so speedy and habitual as to seem almost instinctive and those who practice news gathering are as defensive of scrutiny of the practice as they are of the practice itself" (p. ix). The Glasgow group's (1980) updated work concludes that "'ritual tasks' are ingrained in the professional culture of news organizations and journalists" (p. 398).

Wanda Siu (2009) found that the *Wall Street Journal* and the *New York Times* both supported the tobacco industry against the surgeon general's report about the danger of tobacco in 1964. Although support from the *New York Times* has fizzled over five decades, this is not true of the *Wall Street Journal*. As a newspaper committed to financial rather than civic interests, the *Journal* privileged the economic considerations of tobacco, indicating that ideology plays a role in the way the *Wall Street Journal* works to construct reality in the capitalist world. Journalism as secondary pursuit continues into the modern exploration of the craft. Journalism in terms of traditional roles like gatekeeping and agenda setting are less important than speed, hypertext, and multimedia (Deuze & Paulussen 2002). Joseph Turow (1997) took this idea a step further, predicting that the ease of connecting an audience with advertising will lead to low-income and minority groups' being underserved by media organizations.

Michel Foucault (1970) found discourse to be a key element in understanding a work dynamic. The idea of discourse—a systems approach to work and its organization—may produce a way of thinking about one's function within an organizational dynamic, and the power to define these roles becomes a means of controlling workers. This can be seen as a situation in which the underlying conditions of a worker's actual function are different from the function that the individual perceives; moreover, these conditions change over time. Further, Pablo Boczkowski (2004) and Mark Deuze (2007) both suggested that journalists are in danger because that which has historically been associated with their professional identity is being replaced.

From all these observations, it would appear that the specific discourses of objectivity, such as presenting conflicting truth claims, presenting evidence, presenting the most material facts first, and carefully separating fact from opinion are *rituals* to newsworkers. Through the ritualistic behaviors of professionals, one gains a hint of what may be the deeper function of the newsworker's world. Ritual, though social in its practice, has great utility in the exploration of the individuals who practice it.

Newsroom journalists practice *Ritual* with a capital *R*. Durkheim (1912/2008) observed almost 100 years ago in his classic *The Elementary Forms of Religious Life* that power lies in that which is held sacred. Just as Durkheim's totems, or what can be thought of as divinity, are transformative, perceived as real, and an expression of self for Aboriginal peoples, newsworkers believe that through their rituals and practices, their work can transform society. That these practices are often considered sacred has in the past been advantageous to organizations in that newsworkers performed them as part of a strong business model. These influences on the newsworker are a part of the fabric of the culture; however, they do not wholly explore individual agency or the autonomy built into that culture.

SOCIAL CONTROL AS A COLLECTIVE DYNAMIC

The alternative way to view the individual level of influence is as a lateral consideration rather than in terms of superiority or inferiority to more macro views. Hardt and Brennen (1995) examined the underexplored history of newsworkers and the importance of such work in the United States:

> Traditional press historians have concentrated primarily on the structure of the institution and its major forces, as well as on the

importance of protecting content, instead of addressing the issues of production in terms of labor and newsworkers. They have done so under ideological conditions that have generated a top-down history of the press that privileged property and ownership at the expense of an understanding of news work. (p. ix)

As individual influence has been further explored, many scholars have returned to gatekeeping as an expression of newsworker autonomy. Daniel Berkowitz (1990) attempted to refine White's gatekeeping metaphor and explained that decision making is a group process; thus, content is shaped by group dynamics. When equating journalistic routines and practices with group dynamics, the idea of ritual may again have some benefit. After all, what is ritual? Eric Rothenbuhler (1998) offered the following general but substantive definition of *ritual* to inform communication research: "Ritual is the voluntary performance of appropriately patterned behavior to symbolically effect or participate in the serious life" (p. 27). He further explained that this behavior must be logical and have effects beyond the behavior itself. It must include formal rules, and the symbolism should be explicit. In communication, all players in the ritual accept that participation is symbolically meaningful and effective.

Domingo et al. (2008) found a unique relationship between newsworkers and audiences when looking at audience participation. In European and American newspapers, they found that newsworkers retained decision-making power at each point of production and that they were the final arbiters of audience-driven material. Moreover, Domingo (2008) examined online newsrooms and discovered that interactivity in newsroom discussions was common; the tendency was to consider the audience passive rather than active.

Most content is symbolic, and news, entertainment, print, broadcast, and other media are remarkably similar in that constraint. Organizational contexts are at work on practitioners and on the ways they carry out activities and characteristics related to their roles, crafts, and occupations. Each value, both core (journalistic) and imposed (organizational), may be interpreted in a fashion similar to the way Durkheim viewed the totem. Ideas have the same function within respective spheres. The totem was to Durkheim a stopping point for universal power (*manna*), sacred in its manifestation, real in its influence, but ambiguous enough to serve many functions and the needs of many societies. This universal dynamic explains coalescence for groups that need to function effectively together.

Deuze (2007) found that changing technology, specifically in a digital environment, is not a disparate factor influencing news work in a uniform way; rather, the dynamic must be viewed in terms of implementation and in terms of how it enhances or limits pervious practices and routines. Boczkowski's (2004) study of online newspapers found that organizational structure and work practices determine the ways in which news work adopts technology.

Certainly, individual newsworkers live and work in a social world. Berger and Luckmann (1966) suggested not only that reality is constructed by social interactions to build meaning but also that this meaning depends on the way people interact with each other. Thus, those things that society sees and hears in media provide a symbolic reality for the social world. This approach shows far less regard for the ideology noted in the previous section and finds collective understanding more informative. Graham Murdock (1973) has been clear that those in power influence media; however, he and Peter Golding (1991) warned that this influence could be oversold. "Consumption practices are clearly not completely manipulated by the strategies of the cultural industries but they are equally not completely independent of them" (p. 164).

Bonnie Brennen (2001) reinforced the general idea that journalists are motivated by a social component. The oral histories that she collected from the staff of the *Rochester Democrat* in the 1950s and 1960s attest a sense of higher social function among the rank-and-file newsworkers of the time. And although political activism from the right was a consideration within management (particularly Frank Gannett), there also existed a profound sense of fellowship and respect for those in the lower echelons. One of Brennen's informants described this:

> Frank Gannett himself was far to the right of his editorial staff and far to the right of his editorial writing staff ... however, in Frank Gannett's day, he was very paternalistic. That word was made for Frank Gannett. He used to give out turkeys and have parties and picnics. His wife used to come and she treated us like family. We didn't think in those days he was looking down on us or patronizing us ... but paternalism is rejected out of hand these days. (Brennan, 1995, p. 4)

This informant indicated that not only were the political relationships more tolerant, but the social stratification was less rigid as well. The implied patron-client relationship whereby the patron provides for client with full recognition that he or she would not be functional without the client is indicative of midcentury newsrooms. However, the influence of capital and the power of advertisers were in the front of the typical newsworker's mind. Even then, covering influential businesses, store openings, ribbon cuttings, and the like was prominent practice. But mentioning products in unrelated stories could cause arguments. This was where the power of the gatekeeper came into conflict with the concept of hegemony.

That an institution with an ideology based in service to society finds itself yielding to economic agendas may seem at odds with common sense, but Antonio Gramsci (1840/2000) explained that cultural hegemony arises in every aspect of life. Hegemony is the active dynamic process that allows high social classes to dominate others. It comprises societal norms that are perceived as universal truths about the way things are. Hegemony enters every aspect of daily life and influences work, leisure, and interpersonal relationships. It influences creative energies, thoughts, beliefs, and desires. It creates a status quo, limits alternatives, and contains opportunities. Most important, it shapes public consent so that the granting of legitimacy to dominant classes appears spontaneous and normal in the structure of society.

Hegemony as a collective dynamic transitions the focus of this chapter to another way of looking at social controls in news production. The proposal is that collective decisions meet broad needs and move away from models that privilege power elites as those who pull all the strings. Hegemonic discourse is bigger than the media elite and includes ideas such as objectivity. An alternative theory regarding routines of news production suggests that the media are in fact disconnected from the bourgeoisie and their control mechanisms because the latter need the media to confirm their legitimacy (as a civic force) in the capitalist system (Hallin, 1985). News gatherers cannot become purely ideological instruments of those in power, for this would harm their credibility with audiences. This social constructionist theory asserts that ruling classes are not as powerful as previously stated, and newsworkers have at least some liberty in their selection and presentation of news (Molotch & Lester, 1974).

Marilyn Greenwald and Joseph Bernt (2000) addressed the extramedia and ideological levels of influence by considering the changing cultural atmosphere of the news-gathering world. They noted, "[M]any news consumers view the press not as a watchdog that monitors huge faceless corporations, but as one of those huge impersonal corporations" (p. 3). They also explained that the issue is not so simple:

> It [disenchantment with the media] derives instead as a result of numerous complex changes in society and the media over the last two or three decades. Changes in four aspects of American society —in its economic system, recent legal rulings, culture and technology—have had both subtle and obvious effects on news content and consumers (p. 3).

In the 1990s, many staff members at news organizations were unlikely to have lived long in the city where they worked owing to the decline of local ownership. "The result was readers and viewers [who] were increasingly isolated from their local newspapers and television stations" (p. 6). "Inevitably, changes outside the newsroom affect the culture within the newsroom, thus shaping how news is presented" (p. 9). Greenwald and Bernt explained that influences on news values centered on the changing techniques of news gathering; they noted that computers and the Internet promote a culture of desk reporting.

Tuchman (1976, 1978) found social construction only loosely related to power; moreover, she contended that the social construction of the "factual world" has more to do with the strategic rituals (such as objectivity) that allow newsworkers to do their complex jobs within the news cycle. She found this telling in terms of how they construct reality. Stuart Hall (1999) found the assignment of meaning and reality personal: journalists use authoritative sources to create conceptual maps that organize information and fixed meanings; however, there is no single meaning, and any meaning at all varies depending on the historic, cultural, and personal viewpoints that give them context. Anthony Giddens (1984) argued that institutions do not create discourse; rather, they render those discourses favorable and legitimate in the eyes of the public by controlling the allocation of resources through the economic forces under their influence. This indicates that the discourse at least originates with the individual journalist, but under social constraints.

Other scholars have found the newsworker's individual level of influence even more profound. Erving Goffman (1974) asserted that the social construction of reality is an act of participation between media performers and the audience. He used the metaphor of a theater to explain that individuals are like actors performing scenes in front of others, and the stages are media that allow communication to be framed. Todd Gitlin (1980) explained that media frames allow the newsworker to organize material in a way that can be disseminated cleanly to the public and organized in the production process. It was in this way that news became a symbolic construction of social reality. In these instances, Goffman and Gitlin have presented social construction as a value-free manifestation of what media do rather than quantifying them based on their influences. Robert Entman (1991) supported this position, evaluating the ways the U.S. media frame international news events. Several players are involved in affecting whether news is acted upon, understood, remembered, or even noticed, including the narrator, the reporter, and the authoritative voices and sources quoted by him or her. Gamson, Croteau, Hoynes, and Sasson (1992) found an optimistic voice among media. They noted:

> If all we have learned is that reality construction takes place in a commercialized space that promotes a generalized "feel good about capitalism," this does not take us very far. It leaves open a bewildering array of messages that are produced in many voices and many modes and that can be read in many different ways. Whatever we can learn from reality construction by examining the process, it leaves a great deal open and undetermined. (p. 380)

The many voices of media can often be read oppositionally, and the media world is a site of a struggle in which the powerful are forced to constantly justify why their views of reality should be dominant and accepted by the masses. This dynamic undermines the power-influence nature of media discourse and allows room for other voices—including that of the individual newsworker—to offer competing constructions of reality on an individual level.

The Social Realities of the Newspaper World

According to de Botton (2014), news is everywhere. It is an almost inescapable living entity that finds its consumer with remarkable swiftness. The tight ecology between the production and consumption of news has caused consumers and journalists to change.

Synthesizing the theoretical underpinnings of the newsworkers' world through different theoretical positions makes clear that the idea of the newsworker as an influence has often been challenged, but it has also been shown to be profound in many ways. This study thus required an analytical tool through which to observe macroinfluence dynamics in order to determine whether and how newsroom culture can be considered influential. One such tool is ethnographic fieldwork. According to Antonius Robben and Jeffrey Sluka (2007), ethnography is the response to a desire to advance human understanding; the potential for its application exists in every culture and subculture. In cultural anthropology, the dominant tool is fieldwork based on participant observation, which hinges on the dynamic and contradictory synthesis of subjective insider and objective outsider. As an insider, the fieldworker learns what behavior means to the people themselves. As an outsider, the fieldworker observes, experiences, and makes comparisons in ways that insiders would not (p. 2).

The synthesis to which Robben and Sluka referred arises not only from cultural differences but from cultural change, as well. The change that is taking place in the social and professional climate of today's newsroom is weighty indeed. A newsroom community, like any other community, faces unique issues. The pressures involved in observing a community have been addressed by Gerald Berreman's (1967) "Behind Many Masks," in which he noted that "in terms of community, social orders are always stratified, plural, and internally divided, and relations have to be maintained with different factions and interest groups who may be in conflict or competition with each other" (p. 136).

The way newspapers were operated and conceptualized for most of the 20th century still lives and is strong in the American mindset; however, it has been undergoing a dynamic paradigm shift over the past two decades. Technology and the profit motive have led to layoffs. This raises questions concerning how threatened livelihoods affect journalistic autonomy, job performance, story choice, the newsworkers' treatment of stories, and the division of responsibility.

One justification for an expansive look at social changes within newsroom organizations can be seen in Herbert Gans's articulation of the fundamental differences between the "golden age" and the modern age of journalism: "Journalists were thought to be different ... coming from the working class, less elitist, [they] were not paid or treated like celebrities. Staffs and budgets were larger as well, and the world, like the country, was dotted with well-staffed bureaus" (p. xvi). Gans insisted that virtually all national news organizations continued to swear by objectivity and that journalists still aimed for fairness and detachment. These values, generally considered to be positive attributes of journalists, according to Gans, were at odds with the goals of stakeholders. "[Journalists] do not comprehend the persistence with which ideologues pursue their objectives, play hardball politics, and refuse to compromise, but then they don't see how their own professional values constitute an ideology" (p. xviii).

What does this indicate about personal values, human and social considerations, power within the newsroom, and internal stakeholders? Gans concluded that clichés with regard to the justification for multiperspective news (or news with more than one focus) are somewhat flawed. He rejected the ideas that democracy rests with a well-informed public and that knowledge is power; rather, he noted that "journalists themselves see this function as valuable" (p. 332). In regard to media organizations, he suggested that American journalists share a set of "enduring values" that shape the nature of news. He discovered that in the conventions of the news story, order and the presentation of its narrative structures have been shown to shape not only what becomes news but also how it is presented.

The inception of the Telecommunications Act of 1996 opened opportunities for journalists to reach communities in new ways (Aufderheide, 1999). The medium of the Internet was young, the possibilities for digital communication untapped. In time, the Internet itself permanently eliminated a substantial source of newspaper organizations' revenue, classified advertising (replaced by online forums such as eBay, Craigslist, etc.). This shift has had detrimental effects on the bottom line and on staff members at many newspapers, but audiences still look to newspapers to serve their information needs.

> The news media that have been losing audiences have also lost income from advertisers, and the result is smaller budgets and slimmer news organizations. New technology induces further downsizing ... like other American businesses, news firms are now demanding higher profit margins. (Gans, 2004, p. xii)

The idea of a cultural study of newsworkers is not new. Returning to the work of Warren Breed, I note that he explored pressures and organizational stresses prior to the Internet's rise and the digital revolution. His groundbreaking study of social control in newsrooms is considered one of the first explorations of newsrooms as the locus of a unique subculture. Breed compiled his analysis from 120 interviews of newsworkers. He concluded that social control and policy are maintained through a series of structural and behavioral norms. Breed's use of interviews as a method represents one of several ethnographic tools that social science uses to examine cultures. Although Breed's analysis is decidedly cultural and based on community structures, he never used the word *ethnography*. Much of his work was informed by his years as a journalist, and he did not frame it as participant observation. Breed concluded that policy sometimes supersedes journalistic norms, that staffers often personally disagree with it, and that executives could not legitimately demand that policy be followed. Breed termed policy *controlling behavior*. In the newsroom, such behavior includes intuitional authority and sanctions, feelings of obligation and esteem toward superiors, collegial relationships with authority, mobility aspirations, absence of conflicting group allegiance, the pleasant nature of the activities, and news itself becoming a "value" as a civic function.

According to Hanno Hardt (1990), the loss of autonomy was technological in origin. He explained that the drive toward technological optimization required that a work force to be able to perform many functions and adapt quickly. This increased control over journalistic products at the expense of creativity and intellectual discourse. According to Simon Cottle (2003), "the social contextual realities of news production deserve attention because they lie between the economic determinations of the marketplace and the cultural discourses within media representations" (p. 13).

This development raises the following question: What personalities and values are involved in the newsroom now? Underwood (1993) cited opinions of newsworkers and former newsworkers whose statements attest themes such as these: Profit does not have a place in the running of a newsroom, *USA Today*–style "McPapers" do not sell well, and finally, "newsrooms must often institute tough newsroom management systems in order to bring along newsworkers' reluctance to buy into the philosophy of market-oriented journalism ... a lot of the fun [went] out of journalism when it became a product" (p. 38).

Underwood revealed that even editors see systems management as overly focused: "fashion[s] in managerial styles come ... they blow, and they go"; editors are not editors anymore but managers, and modern corporation management is sapping the vitality out of creative editors and reporters. Underwood concluded that the components that make journalism special and important "can be cheapened but are somewhat indelible" (p. 176). "The new corporate minded editors say they are giving people what they want, yet they do not really know what they want. Surveys can be read a number of ways and that is why they have done the newspaper business so little good" (p. 176).

Research Questions

The world of the modern newsworker is convoluted. Traditional concerns and craft skills within a newsroom culture have not in any way dissipated with the advent of digital products, but those digital products have yielded few new jobs and have added new levels of process in which newsworkers must engage within a brief news cycle. Moving or elimi-

Influence Within and Beyond 31

nating personnel has amplified this stress. Newsworkers struggle with communication in the office and with understanding corporate directives. At the same time, understanding these directives does not guarantee that newsworkers will agree with them. In fact, it normally means the opposite, for these directives are often regarded as the poor conclusions to badly designed research. Corporate directives are often seen as operating contrary to long-practiced routines that have advanced and supported the civic mission of journalism.

The foregoing literature review reveals that the social construction of reality has many interpretations, but it also indicates that the concept has great potential to inform the reality of the modern newsroom. Potential influences on newsworkers are plentiful, and the literature does not attest a consistent hierarchical pattern regarding what newsworkers find influential or what they might identify as priorities. The remainder of this volume addresses the ways newsworkers internalize and act upon these considerations and seeks a deeper understanding of newsworkers' reality. Given the limitations of the research cited in this chapter, this study explores the following research questions.

> 1. How are news values socially constructed in light of the digital paradigm in journalism and the pressures emerging from changing platforms, economics, or other external issues? How are they reconciled with the traditional civic roles of the press?
>
> 2. Can the observations of newsroom journalists be categorized into consistent themes to facilitate a better understanding of the profession's reality, and if so, what new or old mechanisms and routines are in place to ensure that individual motivations are organizationally favorable?
>
> 3. How are disconcerting influences received, perceived, and acted upon by newsworkers?

4. How are current newsroom climates, extramedia concerns, and ideology manifest in the newsroom, and how do they affect morale?

5. How are collegiality and autonomy in the current newsroom environment challenged or changed? What motivates these behaviors?

6. How do newsworkers view the goals and direction of journalism, and are the concerns and values of newsworkers informed by traditional newsroom routines?

7. Are individual passions infused into news work? If so, what is important to newsworkers, and what does that say about those who are attracted to the profession?

8. If ritual patterns arise from newsworkers, are they consistent with Rothenbuhler's definition of *ritual*? What elements are consistent with the approaches discussed in the literature, and are they related to the pressures emerging from changing platforms, economics, or other external issues?

Considering the research questions at hand, as well as the aforementioned literature on the social construction of reality, I determined that an amalgamation of several methods of qualitative research was optimal for this project. Paul Leedy and Jeanne Ormond (2001) have discussed qualitative research in terms consistent with the intricate social nature of this study:

> To answer some research questions we cannot skim across the surface. We must dig deep to get a complete understanding of the phenomenon we are studying. In qualitative research, we do indeed dig deep: We collect numerous forms of data and examine them from various angles to construct a rich and meaningful picture of a complex, multifaceted situation. (p. 147)

This research was conducted in newsrooms, and the complexities of vocational issues were germane to understanding the work dynamics. A qualitative and ethnographic approach was chosen for this study because it allowed me to be responsive and watchful in a busy newsroom environment. This study was conducted in two phases, an interview phase and an observation phase; the complete methodology is outlined in the appendix.

CHAPTER 3

THE PROCESS OF NEWSPAPER NEWS WORK

The flow of a typical newsworkers' day can vary greatly from one organization to the next, as well as from one job to another. This chapter is intended to familiarize newcomers with the industry and to highlight broadly accepted changes that have occurred during the past few years. De Botton (2014) noted of one global news organization, "More data flows into the building in a single day than mankind as a whole would have generated in the twenty-three centuries between the death of Socrates and the invention of the telephone" (pp. 251–252). This chapter is not doctrine; however, in the process of performing newsroom jobs, certain activities must invariably take place in order to produce a piece of consumable journalism for the public.

The newsrooms examined in this study were typified by an open bay of desks or cubicles and televisions tuned to CNN or to one of the local news channels. At one operation, each assignment editor had his or her own mini TV tuned to local news, as well as televisions mounted overhead and throughout the newsroom broadcasting national stories. At a smaller operation, the newsroom had only one television around which staff gathered to see the breaking national news of the day. Information gathering is the key first step to any newsroom function.

Workers move around their newsroom to communicate with each other as a matter of routine throughout their days. They do this to ask questions about topics that range from deadline concerns to community history, from sources to events of common interest. They keep mementos like bobbleheads and Star Wars action figures on their computer monitors. They often have photos of pets or family framed or pinned to their bulletin boards next to correspondence or news clippings. Birthday cards and balloons remain on desks long after the events have passed, and sports memorabilia can spill over the side of a desk, building up over many years. Some newsworkers use the space under their desks for filing old newspapers. Sometimes this space becomes so full that they cannot even put their legs under their desks to work. At the end of some long days, workers go home and try to have a personal life.

All this is indicative of the typical newsworkers' world as it was observed during this study. It is within this world that newsworkers do their jobs, interacting with sources, management, technology, and one another. This can be stressful, but it is not unlike many other stressful professions. The unique nature of news work comes in the form of its civic function and in the newsworker's role as the eyes and ears of the public. They are government and business watchdogs and must take on all the ethical concerns that such a role entails. It is within that role that the dynamic becomes complex. Although these roles represent the core values of journalism, the organizations for which journalists work have the added goal of running a viable business. Sometimes the watchdog role and the profit motive clash.

Informants for this study consistently explained that there have been immense changes to their jobs over the last several years as organizations have committed to a shift toward endeavors in digital journalism. This includes website management, applications for smartphones and tablets, and the agility to adapt to new platforms as they evolve.

The Process of Newspaper News Work 37

Changing technologies, business concerns, and a shrinking work force challenge formerly naturalized processes—that is, processes that existed before the digital paradigm and that are still required to do news work.

To understand the culture of news work, it is beneficial to first understand the mechanics of the tasks and the practical motivations of those involved in the work. These include new challenges, changes, and struggles in the modern industry, as well as long-practiced tasks. A brief look at the mechanics of day-to-day news work and an exploration of what led many newsworkers into the field inform an understanding of their concerns for the profession and themselves. Further, a look at the areas of new technology that have emerged, as well as consideration of a challenged business model, will lead to a better understanding of the operational directives that influence the workplace. This chapter is not intended as a comprehensive presentation of newsroom tasks; rather, it provides a broad overview of responsibilities germane to this book and supplies context for those who are unfamiliar with the newsroom environment.

THE MECHANICS OF NEWSROOM OPERATIONS

Most operations start each day with an understanding of purpose. This often takes the form of individual news meetings where reporters talk with editors about the stories on which they are working. For some, this meeting may be a formal critique session assessing the prior day's endeavors. In many cases, both occur and can be stratified by position—top editors critiquing and line editors planning content. This dynamic can be thought of as the birth of the day's controls, controls that will allow the next day's materials to reach an audience on time and as expected. These meetings affirm goals and organizational direction. They allow editors to give input to reporters about sources and coverage. This is an extremely naturalized process, and that was as true for Warren

Breed in 1955 as it is now; the process has existed in one variation or another ever since daily newspapering began in the 1700s (Eadies, 2009).

What is new is that digital journalism has dramatically influenced this process and has changed the meaning of *breaking news*. Eight of 10 Americans say the Internet is a significant source of news in their lives (Pew Research Center for People and the Press, 2008). In an international survey of newspaper leadership, 48% of editors said they believed that most people would be reading news online in 10 years (World Editors Forum, Reuters, Zogby International, 2008). In terms of story treatment, immediacy at a newspaper once meant that the next day's edition of the paper would include a story about events that occurred between news cycles. This is not as true in the digital age. Digital specialists upload stories minutes after they are written, as fast as information can be confirmed. This often happens before a story is fully formed, forcing reporters to routinely change stories online as new facts are uncovered.

Digital specialists watch the online traffic and the performance of their organization's materials, and they adjust placement of content to gain as many page hits as possible from readers. These specialists comb the Web and wire services to cultivate material, bring it to the paper's website, and link it to related content. They update social media with promotions and teasers to draw audiences to their pages and represent the organization by reacting to comments left beneath online stories and on social media sites. Although some newsrooms have specifically dedicated breaking-news reporters or breaking-news teams, most reporters and editors contribute content to online media on their own. This takes place outside the traditional processes of news structure but often includes the traditional players, such as copy editors and reporters. Digital specialists at organizations that can afford them fall outside these traditional processes, and jobs in this area are growing even though newsroom staffs are shrinking.

Reporters must find the time to create their stories within an unforgiving news cycle, observing formal and informal deadlines. This, of course, includes much more than writing. They must follow leads, gather facts, call or sit down with sources, and assign photographs or graphics to supplement their work. Having smaller staffs in newsrooms means that reporters are pressed to write more stories, but the depth of those stories often suffers as a result of this increased demand. Reporters must justify the time and subject matter of their work to superiors and carefully evaluate how executives will receive their stories. One reporter observed during this study said that he feels he has the process under control, at least in terms of his organization. He explained that a story is front-page material only if it involves a trend that can subsequently be built upon. He felt this gave the organization a sense of owning the idea. Although this reporter was making an informal and personal observation about what his leadership tends to prefer, all newspapers owned by chains or corporations create operational directives for coverage (explored later in this chapter).

Communication is key to putting out a news product, and newsrooms have tried and tested mechanisms to ensure that all the key players understand expectations and story status throughout the process. Newsrooms create lists of stories called *budgets*. These are working headlines and brief descriptions of stories on which reporters are working. These descriptions exist in a database accessible to all editors and staff. Newspapers owned by chains often have their budgets available to their sister papers, along with stories, photographs, and supplemental materials. There are also often regional partnerships whereby papers with disparate ownership will share stories and resources in an attempt to cut overhead. Budgets include all the elements that will be incorporated into the final story, such as photographs, breakout boxes (fact lists or contact information), graphics (maps or charts), and sidebars (smaller supplemental stories). The budget allows editors and page designers to plan space in the next day's paper and to decide whether holding a story for a later time is in order. The budget is gathered from wire services, reporters, press releases, and press conferences and is usually compiled by a midlevel line editor, although this responsibility normally does not fall to only one person. Depending on the size of the organization, one person is normally the final arbiter (with significant input from editors and reporters) of the budget. Generally, these line editors' responsibilities include making assignments and checking on the progress of stories, listening to emergency scanners, and watching local television broadcasts to make sure nothing is missed. Reporters often have semiprivate queues on local servers that allow editors to view the progress of unfinished work.

Meetings are also key communication tools for journalists, but the models for these meetings vary greatly from organization to organization. Some groups have adopted a culture of fewer meetings, using e-mail for immediate communication. E-mail messages are so much the norm at some sites that in-boxes rarely leave computer desktops as work is completed, and reporters keep mobile devices close for quick e-mail access. In one newsroom observed for this study, there was little distinction between e-mail and instant messaging, for workers responded to e-mail messages as fast as they appeared in their in-boxes.

Regularly scheduled meetings, set in stone, are the norm for some newsrooms. At these meetings, editors and other staff plan front-page stories for the upcoming weeks, and departments meet as enterprise-reporting teams, government-reporting teams, or design teams. The meetings observed for this study tended to be extremely informal; individuals came and went as they pleased. The number of newsworkers involved in any given meeting varied with the size of the newspaper. Larger papers had meetings of about seven people (such as an entire night-design team), and about once a month an all-staff meeting conducted by the executive editor would take place. Some operations were so small that meetings were attended by only one person and an editor, or they were frequently canceled. Staffers at the small operation indicated that meetings were a holdover from a time when staff had been more plentiful and robust. The staff had gone away, but the routine remained. Newsworkers at meetings were often as engaged with their smartphones as they were in the meetings.

At some point, the news gatherers must hand off their work to news presenters, who are charged with quality control, amalgamation, and the presentation of material. In other words, they read stories and put them on the pages, but this is a deceptively simple way of describing the work for which news presenters are responsible. Within this function reside remarkable complexity and accountability. Presenters design pages, among other duties, but the titles of these newsworkers and their specific duties vary from place to place (copy editors, designers, and paginators, to name a few). Some organizations may have copy editors devoted only to reading copy and designers who only design pages, but often these tasks are performed by one and the same person.

Each day presenters receive different numbers of stories of varying length that include various components. They must assess page dummies (the blank pages with advertisements placed on them) and plan the placement of stories. The number of pages, number of advertisements, and configuration of those advertisements fluctuate with each day's edition, as do the length of the stories, the shape of the art elements, and the number of those elements. At the same time, presenters try to reflect design theory and the publication's individual design philosophy while honoring requests made by editors and those on the gathering side of the operation. They also must plan to incorporate breaking news that can quickly tear the best plans asunder. The function of copy editing is the duty of presenters. These professionals must be versed in media law (such as laws regarding libel) and proficient in grammar and the organization's writing style guidelines (such as Associated Press style). They must have strong institutional and community knowledge and be good interpreters of a reporter's intended meaning.

All these matters must be addressed before pages are sent to print.

All this is done within what is normally an eight-hour work cycle.

As the printed news product has become smaller, the responsibilities of design desks have not. Not only must production workers often upload digital content during their production window, but the industry is transitioning local departments into regional or national design centers. These design centers must handle the pagination of several of the organization's properties, often in different states. These transitions are brutal in that staff members are laid off or forced to relocate. Those who remain at the site must manage the flow of pages in the traditional way until the design centers are ready. Some workers are laid off just in time to see temporary workers brought in to do their old jobs until the transitions are complete.

Breaking News and Digital Dynamics

As mentioned earlier, the online component of daily news organizations has had a profound impact on the routines of journalists and on the way these organizations are staffed and structured. Many organizations have shifted resources away from their printed newspapers in favor of digital products. Newsrooms have lost revenue to online competitors and have invested heavily in getting some of that money back. They have done this by charging individual newsworkers or online specialists with increasing online value. This takes several different forms. Programmers create digital products, such as new online pages that offer information or services different from those available in the traditional print formula. These online pages often go beyond standard online news pages and may include community guides with maps, restaurant guides, or traffic reports. Administrators call such pages *products* and the advertising space therein *inventory*. The goal is to create as many new (not necessarily news) products as possible and to sell the inventory. As these Web pages are created, they must be maintained, and although the goal is to make these pages as self-sustaining as possible, maintenance normally falls to site managers who update information. These tasks do not constitute new jobs and should not be mistaken for industry growth. Rather, these jobs are replacing the traditional craft skills associated with journalism, including writing and photography. Moreover, it is not an equitable trade. Online advertising yields only about 10% of the revenue that print advertising does; thus, newsrooms can no longer support staffs of the size they once did (Karp, 2007). This shift has caused massive layoffs and overwhelming workloads for those who remain. The implication of this for the rank-and-file journalist is ugly and involves a redefinition of the tasks of news work.

A sparse few traditional journalists have reaped the benefit of this new technology in their newsrooms. The ability to digitally upload stories and remotely communicate with editors has allowed a few breaking-news reporters to better merge personal obligations and their workloads. The ability to customize digital products for different geographic areas has, in many markets, done away with several editions of the same newspaper (although much of this continues in areas that are notably different, such as covering discrete state governments). This development has cut newsprint and the work force at the same time. The staff required to put out these editions has been diminished because online specialists can update sites quickly; thus, fewer workers are required.

OPERATIONAL DIRECTIVES

For many years large media conglomerates have been searching for the correct formula for growth in the news industry. Now, faced with shrinking profits, they search for a way to survive. Operational directives are the result of what Underwood (1993) called *market-oriented journalism*. He concluded that audiences respond poorly to it. If this study is any indication, newsworkers like it even less. Operational directives are crucial to understanding the industry today because of their variable nature and their direct influence on news work. It is from the desire to grow and to be appealing that research-driven news directives have sprung, and surveys and focus groups are the key tools of market-oriented journalism. Studies of this sort are meant to create an amalgamation of journalism values (as corporate executives understand them) and to articulate what readers will find appealing. The hope is that as demographics and trends are identified, the markets will grow, and the publications will flourish. These operational directives have had many names over the years that resonate with veteran newsworkers: News 2000, Real Life, Real News, New Information Center, Key Topics, Passion Topics, and so on. One former Gannett editor had this to say about the News 2000 directives implemented before the turn of the century:

> It was an effort to re-structure the newspaper's news content according to reader opinion. That's why we held focus groups asking them what they wanted to see us cover. If I remember, we did make some changes based on that initiative, including some rearranging of beats and adding some new ones. We were looking ahead to all the possible changes in technology and the world that was supposed to happen in the year 2000. (Personal communication, November 2, 2011)

These directives are meant to ensure that organizational research is reflected in the product, but they contain a number of friction points for the average newsworker. Among them are the requirements that reporters include key readership zip codes when calling sources and apply certain desirable demographics in choosing sources for stories. The story may even be written in a manner that puts news favorable to a certain group at the beginning of the article. Directives like this lead newsworkers to resist and resent such orders, but most newsworkers acknowledge that from time to time the research reinforces core journalism values (such as investigative reporting). The idea is certainly that the research serves readers, and marketing these directives gives the impression to readers that they are being served.

Naturally, readers are not privy to what is removed from content or to the possible manifest meanings behind these changes unless they notice these things on their own. One recent organizational push was presented to readers with the ideas highlighted in a front-page letter from the editor. The editor unveiled a redesign that entailed a new look, a new local section, and a renewed emphasis on investigative journalism. She explained that these changes had come after months of research regarding what was important to readers. The issues involved in organizational research are explored further in subsequent chapters, but as an issue of process, they present another level of daily engagement that newsworkers must interpret and incorporate into their work.

The ways newsworkers balance these directives with the other demands of their profession varies. Some newsworkers wholly ignore directives, forcing editors to "cowboy up," as one newsworker called it, and confront the staffer; sometimes they do, but more often they do not. Usually, managers avoid direct confrontation owing to their workload, distaste for conflict, or their own belief in newsworker autonomy. Other times, the directive is simply not strongly emphasized. For example, an editor may tell a photographer, "We would like to see more video on the website." However, the editor will not put a plan in place or will provide no training or quota, creating the impression that the instruction is only lip service to the corporate directive—a directive that the administrator him- or herself may not believe is useful.

The other reason newsworkers may ignore such corporate instructions is that numerous directives come periodically, change often, or are accompanied by many other directives. Newsworkers place other priorities ahead of them, believing they will become obsolete given enough time, that the consequence of ignoring them will be mild, or simply that no one will notice. Newsworkers see these directives clearly and react to them very much as Schlesinger (1978) observed, as nonsubstantive and as merely cosmetic. Sometimes directives are not acted upon because they are seen as pandering or as lowering the civic or cultural function that the newspaper represents. For example, this could be the case when an arts reporter is asked to compile celebrity gossip briefs because they appeal to women aged 22 to 35. In the end, many resist operational directives because they feel those directives hurt the paper or their personal mission as civic-minded journalists and serious professionals.

Other newsworkers see new directives as an ingrained challenge naturalized to the culture. They enjoy the shift in focus and see new directives as representing growth and improving the ways in which readers are engaged. Often these changes open the door for promotions and new job titles. Naturally, newsworkers who accept and embrace directives are positively supported by the organization. These dynamics have changed somewhat since Breed explored them in 1955, although this study suggests that they have been enhanced rather than changed, given that they still exist in their essential forms. The social controls Breed observed in the newsroom are as follows:

1. Intuitional authority and sanctions
2. Feelings of obligation and esteem for superiors
3. Mobility aspirations
4. Absence of conflicting group allegiance
5. Pleasant nature of the activities
6. News becoming a value

Conclusion

News organizations no longer look the way they once did. Empty desks and reallocated spaces are one of the physical manifestations of the digital paradigm. Though there have been some monetary gains in the form of digital subscriptions, philanthropy, and venture capitalism, traditional advertising through print-ad revenues still accounts for more than half the support for professional journalism. And that number dropped 52% from 2003 to 2013 (Pew Research Center, 2014).

Operational directives as they have been observed during this study are veiled in decisions about content but are formed so that organizations can streamline operations. This streamlining means that newsworkers must incorporate more tasks and considerations into their workday.

The Process of Newspaper News Work 47

Organizational directives have changed in the last few years, becoming more overt and digitally favorable, but the overall goals remain the same. The plans themselves are not new. Corporate research departments and independent consultants have for a long time been trying—and largely failing—to advise owners, publishers, and top editors about how to attract readers in certain age groups or geographic locations. What is new is the desperation. Whereas once these plans needed to fit neatly into the core missions of journalism, or at least appear to be a service, now journalism is a craft secondary to any content that will draw readers and online viewers.

The controls put in place to guarantee a product the next day are themselves perhaps slowing workers and adding to an overwhelming work cycle. News presenters are caught in the middle of this paradigm shift, asked to do more and more as staffing is reduced and their own futures appear bleak. Reporters are often equally taxed as layoffs and organizational directives leave them asking how they can produce a news product that is consistent with core values, safe from organizational sanctions, and important rather than merely entertaining.

CHAPTER 4

How Newsworkers See Their World

A significant majority of journalists believe that increased bottom-line pressure is seriously hurting the quality of news coverage. This was the opinion of 66% of national news people and 57% of local journalists surveyed in 2004 (Pew Research Center for People and the Press, 2004). Owing to the nature of the profession, newsworkers are a keenly observant group. They are trained to interpret surface-level communications and people's actions for underlying meaning. Many are adept at digging up financial records and personal information, and they consider it their duty to hold financial stakeholders and the affluent accountable for everything from criminal behavior to social injustice. Existing in the world of journalism means being surrounded by skepticism, and few can argue that the forces at work in society have given newsworkers any reason to set suspicion aside. That newsworkers assess their own organizations in the same terms should come as no surprise. The shift from economic prosperity that has led to layoffs and restructuring has not been embraced by newsworkers as the sole reason for the struggles of the industry. Instead, they see poor leadership as the cause of the existing strife. This chapter explores what newsworkers think of their world and profession, as well as what their personal observations indicate is the direction journalism is taking.

This chapter is guided by in-depth interviews and observations of journalists who have performed a range of newsroom jobs. The hope is that newsworkers' voices will inform an understanding of the culture as it has grown from the newsroom processes reported in the last chapter. The names of informants have been changed to protect their anonymity. The questions (they appear as section headings) are used as signposts for responses, but much information was also gleaned from observations and informal conversations.

It is important to note that as I examined the responses, it became evident that the components of dominant themes were not limited to any particular question. For example, some respondents used the question regarding the value of their publication as a springboard to discuss digital transition, whereas others talked about their personal digital savvy when asked about their plans for the next five years. Though themes are grouped under the questions that the answers most often pertained to, the informant might have been responding to a different question in exploring an emerging theme.

News as a Service: How Do You View the Value of Your Publication for Your Readers?

Ten years ago journalists nationally were divided on the question whether the profession was advancing or regressing; 46% of local journalists and 51% of national journalists thought the profession was heading in the wrong direction. Moreover, there was a significant divide between executives and reporters; 57% of executives saw the direction as positive, whereas only 39% of reporters did (Pew Research Center for People and the Press, 2004). The newsworkers in this study reflected this division in some ways but added context to the dynamic. Newsworkers tend to think first in terms of journalism's civic responsibility. Many indicated that in the face of media overload, their products should be more important than ever for giving context and clarity to readers in a convoluted world. Informants found the services they provided to be unique and often superior to those of other local media and online services not affiliated with their brand. They were also hyperaware that they were struggling to perform these functions with depleted resources and staff. Cathy, a line editor with 27 years of experience at a small daily newspaper, explained her understanding of what she called a "broken business model," which made the newsroom more beholden to advertising than ever, even as advertising dollars were drying up:

> *The newspaper used to be a good watchdog—we used to do a lot of investigative reporting. That's what I see our role as—watchdogs and helping people understand the community. Now we have cut staff and hours so much that we are not doing that anymore. Investigative journalism? I'm trying to think what was the last thing we did that was investigative. Right now we are doing a "jobs package" that is linked to our classified section. That is the closest thing we are doing to investigation.*
>
> *That to me is tragic.*
>
> *We are missing out on investigating things, but we are not even getting regular news covered. It's catch as catch can. If someone is here who knows how to do something, it gets done; if not, whatever. It is a vicious cycle—the economy is bad, advertising is gone, and we can't get it back. The papers are dinky. Classified is decimated. We do not have the money to keep the staff to keep these papers full.*

Opinions such as Cathy's dominated the responses. Newsworkers were often visibly irritated when they reflected on the level of service they were able to provide now compared with the past. Even at publications that had a focus on or a specific team devoted to investigative reporting, individuals were keenly aware that they were not doing nearly as much as they once had.

Some newsworkers saw this difficult time as transitional. Several opinions regarding the shift toward digital media and the future of journalism were positive or at least hopeful. These opinions involved the belief that the corporate-driven research and the directives that follow it would at some point lead to news outlets' finding their audiences again. Redefining newspapers as non-platform-specific information centers was one of the many operational directives in which some newsworkers were placing their hopes. Some informants saw staying on the cutting edge as synonymous with being non–medium specific in terms of the traditional platform (print) and as a plan for reaching a broader audience online. Butch, a line editor with 12 years of experience in journalism who was working at a large metro newspaper, viewed the digital shift and personnel reduction in the following way:

> *Journalism is going through a big transition. I hear a lot in terms of "You can't charge for your product online because people are going to get the information from somewhere else." I think about how in [this city] there is one person who covers city hall, one who covers the county government, a couple of reporters that cover the police ... It is different, but I think the fundamentals are the same.*
>
> *There is a swath of our readers who do not expect to get their news on the end of their driveway; they expect to get it on their phone or on their Blackberry. I think the platform has changed. Certainly the reporting experience has changed with the advent of blogs and community journalism, but the paper has been aggressive. When we have had to lose staff, the staff we have lost has mostly been in middle management ... we could do more with more people, but I cannot honestly sit here and complain about resources in terms of news gatherers.*

REGRETS: IF YOU HAD IT TO DO OVER, WOULD YOU STILL BECOME A JOURNALIST?

In 2013 about a quarter of those who had received bachelor's degrees in journalism or communication said they regretted it (Becker, Vlad,

Simpson, & Kalpen, 2012). The reasons newsworkers chose journalism as a profession are as varied as the jobs within that profession. The overwhelming majority of subjects in this study said that given the option again, they would still choose journalism. However, those responding negatively had strong bitter feelings about the financially driven nature of news production and the recent changes in the way news organizations are structured. Although many newsworkers said they would still become journalists given a do-over, this was certainly not an indication of whether an individual was despondent about the profession.

Most informants told me about their personal journeys through journalism and why they had taken up the profession. These stories touched on several themes, and individual reasons certainly overlapped to some degree. Many of those interviewed said that they had an affinity for or had discovered a talent for a craft associated with journalism. "I loved to write," was a one of the most dominant themes for reporters. Those with jobs other than reporting were likewise enamored of crafts related to a specific skill set, such as taking photographs or editing. These passions had often been cultivated in high school. These newsworkers saw journalism as a way to practice writing or photography, just as a doctor would practice medicine. Justin, a photographer with fourteen years of experience at a small daily newspaper, said this of his direction:

> *I started in photography in high school and started thinking about what kind of pictures I wanted to take. At that time I had a different view of what a professional photographer was or did; I thought the only options were newspapers, magazines, working in a studio, or shooting weddings, and I thought, "I don't want to work in a studio or shoot weddings," so I went into journalism. So, would I do it again? Yeah, I think so, because I still like making the kind of pictures you make as a newspaper photographer.*

The medium itself appeared to have had little meaning for newsworkers in the process of forming a career choice, but few newsworkers encountered in this study had transitioned from other news media outlets to newspapers. There are many indications that this is not true across the industry. Converging newsrooms and organizations in a given geographic area are finding that sharing resources with one another is a good way to cut overhead. Social media and other online products are often rolled together. In terms of traditional newspapers engaging other media, the staff of one small newspaper observed for this study tried to drum up business by doing public access shows with no advertising or other support. This was done in the hope that the paper would profit from the synergy a new platform created. Although it yielded no direct monetary return, it was a creative way to direct journalistic endeavors and was enlivening to those who participated.

Some informants had legacy connections to journalism, having had a parent in the field. Others were a part of journalism's long journeyman tradition. They had found newspaper work a viable option for employment in their hometowns after high school. Interviewees in this group had at one point worked in other departments at the newspaper, such as distribution or printing, and had moved into the newsroom for higher pay and more interesting work or because of an institutional reorganization. These newsworkers certainly tended to be older, but this was not true across the board.

The desire to do something satisfying merged with a sense of citizenship for many newsworkers. Several indicated that they felt a civic duty —some even called it a higher calling—to do news work. These respondents were moved by the social and historic watchdog functions of newspaper journalism and saw their work as way to give voice to the disenfranchised or to make strides toward social justice. Roger, a line editor with 31 years of experience in journalism who was working at a small daily newspaper, explained how social consciousness motivated him:

> When I was in college, I was involved in some social change movements. It was the '60s and early '70s. And I would still like to see more people get involved in whatever is important to them—and perhaps move just a small piece of society forward. I realized a long time

ago that what I'm going to be able to influence is going to be right around me. And so you try to do the best job you can in that sphere of influence. Part of that for me is the newspaper. I try to keep government honest and try to get people together.

LEGACY: WOULD YOU ENCOURAGE A CHILD, GRANDCHILD, OR A YOUTH YOU MENTOR TO ENTER THIS FIELD?

Most sectors of news media have seen cutbacks in news gatherers. Just a few years ago, a third of local journalists said they felt pressure from either advertisers or corporate owners. Thus, one of the most dearly held principles in journalism, editorial decision making, was being breached (Pew Research Center for People and the Press, 2004). Answers to this question came with some qualification, and informants tended to explain their answers in terms of the mentored individual's personal choices. Very few interviewees answered with an unequivocal yes. Further, few informants were positive about the prospect of a youth following in their footsteps, although they explained that the choice was up to the young person.

Those who said they would tolerate such a choice did so for many of the same reasons already noted. They elaborated by citing the social function and importance of journalism, and they highlighted the positive aspects of the job, such as the gratification of seeing one's work in print, being among the first to know about events, and the sense of fellowship prevalent in the environment. One of the most positive responses came from Donald, a line editor at a small daily newspaper with 38 years of journalism experience:

> *I would still encourage people to go in[to journalism]. You know, when I see college students expressing their interest, I'm very hopeful. To me it's something that ... not only validates what I've done my whole life, but I think young people bring a savvy that I never had. They know the different means of delivering messages, and so forth. So the fact they are interested is, I think, reason for real hope that*

the media does have a future. I think people are still interested in news, but I think they're selecting different ways of learning news.

The majority of journalists were not as positive as Donald about the profession. Most interviewees answered with an unequivocal no the question about their children or protégés following in their footsteps; other respondents explained that though the decision would be up to the individual, the profession did not offer a secure future, nor was it a goal worthy of achieving or maintaining. Reasons mentioned for this despondent reaction among younger newsworkers were the money, the hours, and frequent layoffs, whereas seasoned interviewees cited a growing disrespect for the efforts they put forth and the traditional skills they had cultivated over many years. Quite a few felt they were costing upper management too much money, and that their efforts were rarely good enough. The impression was that the industry was slowly sliding away from them. Todd, a copy editor and reporter with 31 years of experience at a large metro newspaper, made comments indicative of this recurring theme:

I think that the newspaper side of printed journalism is going to slowly go away. You know, we're seeing now that newspapers are shrinking because things like Craigslist, Amazon, and eBay are taking away all the classified ads. The opportunity isn't going to be there in print journalism.

As far as the rest of journalism goes, its reliability, credibility, and quality are all being chopped bit by bit and week by week by the onslaught of blogs. Kids believe what they read on the screen more than what they read on the page, and I know that from my kids: they don't even read the newspaper. I'll show them an article I've written and they don't even read that.

My daughter reads books, [and] my son reads graphic novels, but they are just completely glued to the Internet all the time, so I don't think there is going to be an opportunity in this field to make a living. It's a bad way to make a living, and any desire to be involved in the print product is crazy because it's just not going to hold on long enough for kids to make a living. If they want to blog, that's fine, but they should not become disseminators of news—no way.

PERSONAL AMBITION: ALL THINGS BEING EQUAL, WHAT WOULD YOU LIKE TO DO PROFESSIONALLY IN THE NEXT FIVE YEARS?

Training and professional development programs were common in the newsrooms observed in this study. This has been true for several years. About half of local journalists (56%) said they participated in such activities (Pew Research Center for People and the Press, 2004). However, this study also revealed that many newsworkers were willing to leave journalism and all other forms of media work. They cited concerns about money, the hours, a loss of interest, pending retirement, or a combination of these as reasons for an exodus. Other interviewees said that they wanted out of newspapers but would enjoy doing other media-related work. Public relations and Web business development were among the favored choices. Of the newsworkers who said they would like to stay in media but not necessarily in journalism, many also indicated that they would like to participate in other creative endeavors. Some hoped to write books, nonfiction and fiction; one was interested in developing an interactive children's book. Only two interviewees said they would like to climb higher in their organizations, but most newsworkers said that they would like to stay in their current positions and were willing to change as their positions evolved. Some were excited about the field's transition, and others were resigned to their fates. Ron, an online editor with 11 years of experience at a small daily newspaper, exemplified the former view:

> *I guess I would like to be doing what I'm doing now. My job has changed so much in the last 11 years. I've done a lot of different things, and things have changed so much, but still it boils down to—I'm still a journalist, and I don't see that changing over the course of the next five years. Now, how I do that job will change, will continue*

> to change, but the bottom line is I will still be a journalist. So, yeah, five years from now I plan to be doing basically the same things I'm doing now; it will just be different in [terms of] how our customers consume that product of news. That's what's going to change.

Shelly, a features reporter and columnist with more than 20 years of experience working at the same small newspaper also wished to continue, but she was more resigned than enthusiastic. She felt she was submissive to tasks that were no longer appealing to her in a field that was leaving her and her skill set behind:

> God willing, if the paper survives, I'll probably still be here. Maybe it's just laziness, but I would like to still be here. I wish I could go back to a more expanded features role and less of this being pulled in so many different directions. My dream job would be to do my column all the time. I would come up with stories that way, and not have to do things that have to be done. Some of it may be laziness, that I don't aspire to do something else. Every time somebody else has left the paper, I kind of question why I'm still here.

One key to newsworker satisfaction that emerged from this look at professional aspirations is that fulfillment seemed proportional to how creative newsworkers felt they could be in their jobs. Those who wanted to leave in order to write books were expressing a wish for creativity, and even Shelly, who seemed to have lost all passion for her work, longed for the autonomy and self-direction she once enjoyed in her job.

Personal Passion: What is Important To You Personally and Professionally, and How Does It Come Through in Your Work?

This question was somewhat ambiguous for many journalists, but certain approaches to answering the question did dominate the responses. Several informants found the personal and professional importance of their work in improving the human condition, much as

Roger noted in the quote cited earlier. Most approached the question in terms of professionalism and saw the different tasks and functions associated with journalism and the way they performed their jobs as valuable. Others voiced values that are desirable in most professions, such as organizational skills, hard work, and commitment, as standards that they hoped came through to their audiences and peers. The example interviewees set for their families was paramount, according to informants, and it was influential in their approach to their jobs. Liam, a reporter with 32 years of journalism experience who was working for a small daily newspaper, said this about values, family, and work:

> *When you have a family, it all becomes very important—closeness, caring for each other. And those are the things I think I bring to my work. Honesty. The things I want my daughters to learn and to understand and to project in the world are those things. When you write for a newspaper, you represent the things people say, and to do so, accuracy is key. There is a code to it, and I think it's related to having children and having a family, a loving family and being devoted to it. You're devoted to your craft of journalism the same way. It's important to me that I do a good job; it really bothers me if I think I didn't or [if] people say that I didn't. You have to be honest to that, just like you have to be honest with your family and your children—you have to follow them; you have to be concerned with them. The newspaper is the same way. I think those are related; those things are never easy, but there is a sense of accomplishment, just like raising a family.*

Many newsworkers were passionate about their families, as countless other people certainly are, but a range of interests in areas related to journalism, such as politics, business, sports, and entertainment, also dominated journalists' life outside the newsroom. One online specialist refereed soccer games outside of work. Former athletes and sports enthusiasts often became sports writers. This is hardly surprising. However, Donald, the journalist quoted earlier, talked extensively about starting a yurt dealership when he retired (a yurt is a dome-shaped shelter adapted from those of central Asian nomads that functions as a vacation home) and about running the business much like a recreational-vehicle dealership.

The world of news seldom stops for journalists when their shifts end, but beyond the obvious related pursuits, the newsworkers in this study enjoyed activities that ranged from gardening and singing to woodworking and art. According to Donald, the best journalists he has known were able to cultivate their passions on the job and at home.

Journalism Now: What Important Cultural Dynamic in Journalism Would You Like People to Understand?

In 2012, total traffic to the top 25 news sites increased 7.2%; this is almost four times as much as the increase from 2010 to 2011. Fully 39% of people get their news online or from a mobile device; 31% of adults own a tablet, and 35% own a smartphone (Pew Research Center for People and the Press, 2014). The newsrooms in this study were in the process of shifting their paradigm from a traditional print medium to multiplatform delivery systems. This was a messy transition, given that newsworkers often think in terms of engaging print first. Although these newspapers were not abandoning print, they were engaged in creating a multiplatform business model and in scaling back the information offered in print.

The organizations were also contending with a failing business model, and newsworkers saw monetary considerations poised to sever their livelihoods. The fear involved in such an existence was conveyed in nearly every interview and was the most prevalent cultural shift affecting newsworkers in this study. Other cultural issues included cynicism as a shared trait among journalists, the importance of teamwork and building relationships, distrust of the employing organization, and along with that, feelings that the journalists themselves were not respected or valuable to the organization. These last concerns were tied to layoffs, poor pay, and the changing business model.

Several interviewees felt that their traditional skills were underappreciated or misunderstood and that they were occupying space on the payroll that the organization wanted to fill with younger, multiskilled staffers who were more digitally savvy and less costly to employ. Some saw this cultural shift as an exciting new challenge, but others said it was an opportunity to enjoy the last years of their dying trade. Todd, the copy editor with 31 years of experience at a large metro newspaper, said this:

> *The culture has changed a lot in the last three years. Our department has gone from 29 to 13 people. In a sense, we went from being a newspaper that was corporately influenced, run like a corporation, stiff and quiet, to now where it's more like working at a small paper where ideas are free flowing, people are laughing, people are talking across the room.*
>
> *We don't worry about human resources anymore; I mean, I used to get written up. Someone would complain about me to HR. Now everyone jokes about HR. I have a telephone receiver that has no cord but I call it my HR hotline, so when someone says something inappropriate, I grab it and say, "Hello, HR." Three years ago we never would have done that.*
>
> *It's like, people, we're on this ship. It's slowly sinking, [so] let's enjoy it, have some fun, and lighten up a little bit because all that other stuff—it really doesn't matter.*

Most, however, were far from upbeat about Todd's slowly sinking ship. Many interviewees had difficulty understanding the company's business goals, so they did not know how to train for new digital positions, which may offer more security. In fact, they did not know whether they should retrain at all, because the work they were doing was still needed. This disconnect manifested itself in the newsroom in a number of ways. The most common was described as a loss of morale and work ethic among the groups. Greta, a copy editor with 10 years of experience working at a small newspaper who had a family history in newspaper journalism, said this:

> *We are management heavy, and management is looking upward, working to satisfy the people upward. I don't sense management appreciates a work ethic. I don't think it even recognizes it. Partly because of all this overwork, they don't see what the people around them are doing.*
>
> *I observe people around me that are not acting with integrity and do not seem to be called on it. There are people making personal calls and saying they worked overtime, or playing video games. I don't think that is appropriate to do during work.*
>
> *Here is another way of not feeling supported: we have a deadline, and we'll go for weeks at a time meeting it, then we'll miss it by two minutes and there is a memo the next day. No manager has ever watched me do my shift. And if they haven't seen all the things that happen in the last 10 minutes, then I can't take seriously their criticism.*
>
> *So I don't feel particularly respected. I have to build that respect for myself, to be proud when I walk out. And I understand that the people who are making personal phone calls or playing games are reacting to the same feeling of disrespect. And so they feel, "If you don't respect me, I'm not going to do the job." I can't do it that way and sleep at night.*

Conclusion

This chapter, at a macro level, reveals what rank-and-file journalists perceive as influential to their work in newsrooms. The interviews with journalists who perform a multitude of information-gathering and news-processing jobs paint a picture of a changing profession that is becoming difficult to navigate. The depth of the questions and face-to-face interviews add to the honesty and personal nature of the findings.

How Newsworkers See Their World 63

Newsworkers are deeply concerned about their profession, and many offer creative solutions to deal with financial issues and struggles. However, another resounding theme is that management does not care what rank-and-file newsworkers think, nor does management care about their ideas. Moreover, newsworkers do not have a comfortable or safe avenue in which to share these ideas. The concerns and observations of journalists about their modern newsroom speak to other themes, as well. Three dynamics, or friction points, emerged as vital components in the construction of the reality forming around them. All of these relate in some way to the shift toward digital platforms.

The first issue to emerge centers on the collective acceptance of a broken business model, and newsworker informants could not see how their businesses would make enough money to operate in the next few years. Newsworkers could see little indication that leadership had a desire to save the "sinking ship"—or their jobs. The second issue centers directly on the civic responsibility of the press as it exists within the reality of the services newsworkers provide. Some saw the media as a users' market, believing the public is well served by the ability to access news and information on demand, whereas others felt that the role newspapers play in communities is withering, with no better media outlet able or willing to fill the void. Newsworkers perceived the jobs and resources lost to downsizing as frightening and personally damaging.

Job satisfaction in this changing newsroom is the third theme that emerged. Newsworkers were asking themselves whether newspapers are still serving their interests as craftspeople and creative communicators, the implication being that their skills as wordsmiths and creators of useable information are being undervalued as news organizations have begun to privilege digital and technological savvy.

The various sources of influence as defined by Shoemaker and Reese are indeed at work in the modern newsroom. Informants addressed elements of ideology, extramedia concerns, organizational pressures, and media routines in a naturalized way as they talked about their world.

What diverged was the weight individual journalists gave to each of the influences in the form of pressure, stress, or priority in their jobs. Ideology, if journalism itself can be said to be ideological, tends to be at the forefront for newsworkers; individuals showed a sophisticated understanding of and belief in the social and civic functions of journalism in society. Many understood how economic forces have compromised those roles of integrity in the past, but they did not feel particularly compromised by these forces in the present.

The hindrance to their doing their jobs to the fullest was more closely associated with the economic pressures of what many journalists called a broken business model perpetuated by management rather than a broader struggling economy or changes in technology. This economic concern is consistent with Bagdikian's view that dependence on revenue will restrict news content. However, many subjects viewed that restriction as physical rather than ideological in nature. In other words, fewer employees were available to produce good work, and less space was available for that work. These economic pressures also led to the adoption of new routines that are not historically consistent with journalistic talents. One example of this is wordsmiths required to learn how to upload stories to websites, engage social media, or create and edit video. Because there are fewer workers, moreover, these wordsmiths must also field other traditional tasks, such as taking photographs, copy editing, and designing pages. The influences as imagined by Shoemaker and Reese should perhaps be refined in light of this study, each element of influence, regardless of level, becoming concentrated in the newsworkers' world, like material forced through a funnel (see fig. 1).

New routines related to digital tasks lessen the role of management in terms of its ability to direct the work of staff because the time for new and old tasks is constrained within a news cycle that is more packed than ever. One editor described himself as a circus performer, spinning plates and juggling content. This observation, coupled with many administrators' poor understanding of specific jobs, indicates that newsworkers have much more control than some past research has indicated: they determine what their jobs entail. Adherence to changing routines lends credibility to Harvey Molotch and Marilyn Lester's (1974) interpretation of social construction and the notion that power holders are not always the final authority. Newsworkers in this study saw themselves having increasing autonomy in the face of shifting platforms because no one had time to supervise them; thus, individuals were able to interject their personalities more overtly into their work, although they were generally enjoying the work less and did not feel their jobs were safe.

The concerns and values of newsworkers are consistent with traditional journalistic values but are also the result of pressures that emerge from shifting platforms, economics, and other external issues. The reality that newsworkers today face, as observed in this study, is quite different than the reality of the past. Routines have a direct influence on individual journalists, but informants saw these dynamics clearly and were often able to position themselves in a favorable way.

Newsworkers who favored elements of the journalism craft, such as writing or photography, found the technological shift toward digital platforms uncomfortable. Pressure was exerted by organizations to adopt media routines that move away from traditional roles. Informants often enjoyed those traditional roles, which were often the reason they had entered the business in the first place. Digital-related routines did not require the skill sets that many of these workers possessed. This caused resentment that responsibilities were growing while staff sizes were shrinking. Ultimately, these factors have led to poor performance in both traditional and digital areas.

Although several journalists had adopted this new paradigm with enthusiasm, the majority struggled, indicating that newsworkers are resistant, if not impervious, to having their reality constructed for them.

Figure 1. The hierarchical model with the individual as focal point.

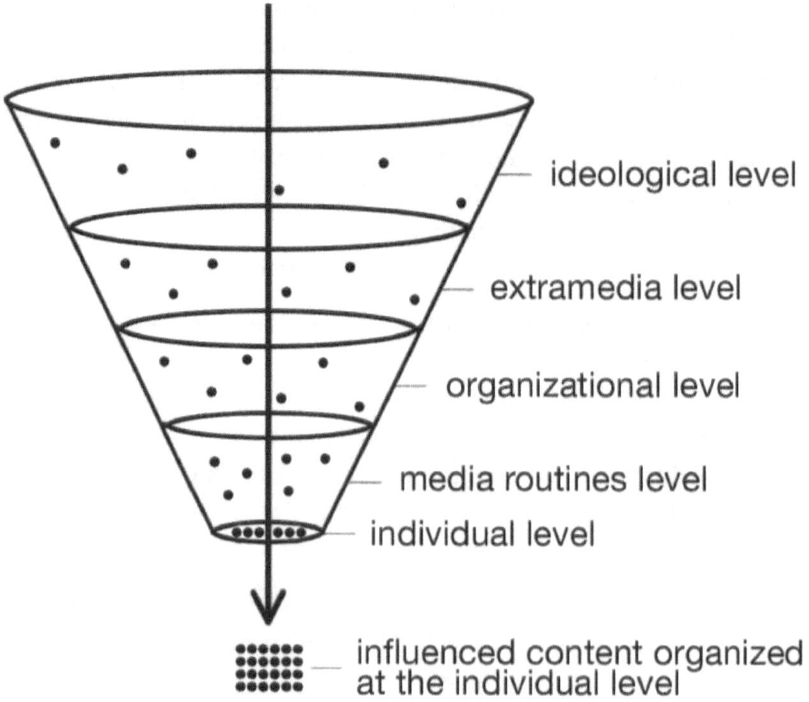

- ideological level
- extramedia level
- organizational level
- media routines level
- individual level

influenced content organized at the individual level

Source. William Schulte (2014), adapted from Shoemaker and Reese (1996).
Note. In this model, each element of influence is pushed through the newsworker's world. Those levels of influence farther from contact with the newsworker create an ambiguous manifestation in the newsworker's routines. These indirect and indefinite influences are symbolized by the spaces between the dots, and influences become increasingly indefinite the more macro an influence becomes. Regardless of level, influence must invariably concentrate itself through the newsworker's work if it is to find an audience. This is like material forced through a funnel. The newsworker is always the final arbitrator of the way this content takes form, being the last to touch the material.

CHAPTER 5

MODERN SOCIAL CONTROLS

As indicated in the preceding chapter, newsworkers see themselves pressed by new digital routines, industry confusion, and the loss of journalistic focus in news organizations. The continuing observations of the industry's culture conducted for this study revealed that these were far from the only occupational pressures and far from the whole story. The issues newsworkers described were, in fact, just a few of the pressures they were dealing with. Warren Breed looked at these issues in terms of social control and policy building and found that policy was often covert in nature.

> Policy, if worked out implicitly, would have to include motivations, reasons, alternatives, historical developments, and other complicating material. Thus a twilight zone permitting a range of deviations appears. (Breed, 1955, p. 332)

The ever-increasing pressures of the modern newsroom have caused management to scramble to direct newsworkers and to struggle with finding a management direction that will have permanence. This chapter, though it does not include every manifestation of policy, explores many prominent social controls and policies, updates the dynamics explored by Breed in a modern newsroom setting, and adds modern controls that were revealed in the participant-observation phase of this study. Excerpts from field notes illustrate and support the assertions.

AUTHORITY AND SANCTIONS MERGED WITH ORGANIZATIONAL DIRECTIVES

Breed reported on an ethical taboo that once prevented policy makers such as publishers from overtly commanding journalists to follow organizational directives. This came about for a number of reasons, but the most influential was an principled idea that journalistic norms are sacred, a trust guaranteed by the U.S. Constitution—an idea that carried weight in its civic function and was manifest in the newsroom. Bringing news to the masses was considered a trust. Policy makers would not have considered meddling in this sacred calling when newsrooms were fiscally healthy. As that health has consistently declined—and sharply declined in past few years—organizations have looked to readership studies to bolster their circulation.

Ten years ago many working journalists were pleased with their management; 65% of national news reporters rated the quality of their leadership as excellent or good, and 53% of local reporters said the same (Pew Research Center for People and the Press, 2004). Now the business office regularly infringes upon those priceless journalistic norms. In the past, organizational directives based on audience research led newspapers to create new beats or new design directives, but core principles remained sacred. Now, in the most desperate of economic times, that meddling taboo has all but disappeared, and a new rule book is being written. In many cases, sanctions on newsworkers for not following organizational directives are much more overt, much more insidious, and much more calculated than Breed indicated in 1955. This is perhaps the result of confusion as to the right direction for news organizations.

Philosophies certainly vary. However, most organizations are looking more closely than ever to readership research to save them in this time of economic need. One instance of this dynamic is attested in the following passage from field notes.

Conflicting Goals

> One week, Sally, an education reporter, planned to write a story and present data from a set of school evaluations being released by the state. When Sally discovered that 12 inner-city schools out of the 22 on her beat had been taken off academic emergency—a status they had struggled to resolve the preceding year—and that there were no significant changes, good or bad, in the suburban schools on her beat, she chose to focus her story mostly on the schools in the city.
>
> She assigned a photograph of a classroom at the school that demonstrated the most improvement. This photo featured a black teacher in a suit teaching with animated hand gestures and black students engaged in the learning process. Sally's story mentioned the inner-city improvements in her lead, mentioned all of the area schools later in the story, and secured space for the reports of all the area schools on page 2.
>
> At the same time Margot, one of the managing editors, had been charged with making sure that suburban areas, which were strong in readership, were served every day by the content of the paper. There were few inner-city readers. Thus, Margot raised the question, "Why did we shoot [photograph] an inner-city school?"
>
> Margot had the story rewritten with a regional focus, the former lead was moved to paragraph five (buried, according to many journalistic norms), and the photograph was replaced with a surplus photograph from a first-day-of-school story that had run earlier that week. That photo was of a white mother hugging her son on his first day of school in one of the suburban communities.
>
> Margot never saw the original photo, nor did she wish to see it.

Sally was subsequently sanctioned for not following policy. The sanction was public and immediate: Margot pointed out Sally's mistake in front of her peers. Margot was visibly angry in the afternoon editors' meeting following the incident. She framed the instance in terms of a reporter unwilling to incorporate into her work the necessary changes called for by the operational model. She said the driving force behind the newspaper was the fact that it is struggling to survive. However, Margot presented even more justification for her actions. She explained that Sally was "just lazy" for not going to the suburban schools, that she had too close a relationship with administration at the inner-city schools, and that she knew better. Sally's peers strongly believed that the story and photo had been more compelling before Margot's changes were incorporated. Margot was performing the directive she had been given, but collegial relationships and Sally's dignity were damaged. It is also remarkable that Margot, an African American, blocked a photograph that featured positive minority representations without having seen the picture.

Esteem for Superiors Meets a Digital Divide

The previous section indicates how the collegial relationships that Breed once observed as a positive aspect of news work have evolved. Relationships between superiors and rank-and-file newsworkers have become strained. Newsworkers have historically viewed themselves with great pride, and many still do (Brennen, 1995). The establishment of expertise, community knowledge, technological knowledge, and quality has in the past made journalists unambiguously valuable commodities. This once encouraged editors and publishers to defer to newsworkers and to depend on them for the details of news gathering and the presentation of the day as they saw fit. It also encouraged them to interact as peers in a collegial and dignified way. This in turn encouraged executives to recognize a symbiotic patron-client relationship. Newsworkers reciprocated in this relationship, seeing their employers paternally, as Brennen described, and giving their best efforts as much for the organization as for the civic trust.

This collegial atmosphere is certainly not extinct, but it is not as prevalent as it once was. Many newsworkers have friendly relationships with their managers, and they may be observed going to lunch together, engaging in friendly conversation, and—perhaps more important—having frank and measured conversations about content choices. However, as noted, the goals of the organization and those of the newsworker often diverge. Much of this rift can be attributed to organizational directives and to directives associated with technology.

Technology has made journalistic craft skills, such as photography, much less mystifying to management. Once, not only were photographers considered masters of focus, composition, and drama, but they were also darkroom technicians and manipulators of film responsible for quality reproduction. The range of skills required to be a good photographer was broad. The age of digital photography has made the transfer and production of images easier. Now management can send reporters into the field with point-and-shoot digital cameras; they return with what is, to management at least, a photograph just as serviceable as the one a staff photographer might have taken. That comparatively few pages are used in daily newspapers themselves, owing to shrinking advertising support, has compounded this devaluing of the photographer, resulting in less need for photographs in print.

Online products have also changed the role of news photographers, who are now asked to produce images for galleries—online groups of photographs documenting a particular event—which are normally composed of the photographer's throwaway shots or taken with the knowledge that they must fill a gallery. Although galleries do get many hits on websites, giving a photographer this task demonstrates to management that a photographer's skills are dispensable, because shooting for a gallery requires little skill. In fact, some galleries are filled with the work of laypeople who happened to attend the event.

In general, newsworkers, not just photographers, are asked to do substantial work in the digital realm. Whereas many professionals have had the advantage of years to master traditional skills and often a college major supported them in acquiring that expertise, newsworkers are now asked to respond to new technology much faster. If newsworkers question the wisdom of the digital direction, are slow to adapt, or have duties that do not allow time for retraining, management frequently labels them as resistant to change, "dinosaurs," or simply not committed enough. Layoffs often result.

Mobility

That there are fewer jobs in the industry means less mobility. As explained in the previous chapter, few newsworkers reported a desire to advance within their own organizations. Mobility in journalism has traditionally served well those willing to move laterally to other newspapers. This was a common source of promotions, as well as a source of raises for those who wished to remain rank-and-file newsworkers; they were often able to negotiate for more money at a different newspaper.

Breed presented the idea that journalism is often a stepping-stone to other media work, but this path is no longer as viable as it once was. Public relations firms and companies that employ public relations professionals at one time valued the experience and insider knowledge that journalists brought to the table. This dynamic has changed somewhat, given that university-level mass communication programs now offer specializations in this area. Likewise, the journalists in this study rarely saw public relations as a comfortable transition.

Although journalists are overall an imaginative group, venues in which to practice journalism outside the mainstream sphere are difficult to find and even more difficult to maintain. Many reporters have said that they would like to practice journalism for themselves but that they feel stuck. Thus, with the shrinking of newspaper operations and the organizations holding all the cards, many newsworkers are desperate to hold on to their livelihoods.

Matters are also difficult for those willing to move up the ladder.

The first step out of the rank-and-file level of news work is middle management. As organizations became top heavy with middle management in more prosperous years, positions like deputy metro editors and assistant features editors were common, but they were also the first positions cut when newspapers became less prosperous (Tourish, Paulsen, Hobman, & Bordia, 2004). In the newsrooms observed for this study, those positions were the first on the chopping block when management restructured for leaner rosters. Cutting unique positions in middle management allowed the ex-employees' tasks to be absorbed by their former supervisors or by the newsworkers whom those middle managers once supervised. It also allowed administration the luxury of ignoring seniority because the positions were unique.

Even with this in mind, some newsworkers still want to move up the newsroom ladder. Individuals must walk a fine line between knowing what the organization will find favorable and how far one can deviate from core principles. Consider the following case.

Matt's Ambitions

> *Matt, a copy desk shift leader at a midsize newspaper, was the only new hire on his organization's copy desk in more than four years. When recounting how he had moved into his current leadership position, he explained that he had taken on extra work whenever possible and listened closely to changing organizational directives to learn where opportunities to get noticed might arise.*
>
> *He made himself instrumental in a directive to improve consistency between several newspapers, as Matt's team was part of the chain's area design hub. This process included Matt's heavy involvement in a redesigned print product and the accompanying research.*

> Matt explained that he generally said yes to company directives and extra work and that he would continue to say yes until it became apparent he would not advance any further in the organization. He saw himself poised to advance as older management structures fell away and gaps in the structure were created. As this happened, Matt wanted his superiors to positively reflect on his support and hard work.
>
> Saying yes, however, was not always effective and came with challenges. Matt was at a large meeting involving a content consultant who formally worked for the New York Times, and many editors from the companies' different properties.
>
> The meeting was an instructional session on how to report to readers the internal processes newspapers engage in as they gather information for in-depth reporting packages. This is called process language.
>
> One seasoned editor expressed the opinion that readers were not very likely to care about the process of making the story because they were the story itself. To this the consultant explained that those were not the customers they wished to cultivate. Matt, wanting to add his support to the momentum of the conversation said, "It is like that old business adage, 'Fire your worst customers.'" This comment was a serious faux pas for Matt.

This idea was poorly received in the room. Although Matt had voiced the exact intent of the consultant, "firing readers," or treating them callously, was an affront to journalism norms beyond what could be accepted in this public forum. Consulting agencies in general help news organizations address a number of issues, including redesigning, boosting sales, and training. Many organizations have seen significant circulation boosts that they attribute to consulting (Yang, 2013). However, organizational consultants do have a somewhat nefarious reputation among some newsworkers. Several workers in this study felt that consultants did very little work for their compensation and had a poor institutional understanding when it came to an organization's specific needs. Many did not want to buy in to consultants' assessments of their work or consultants' evaluations. Many journalists have not survived suggested restructuring, and consulting in the past has treated news work like an assembly line (Shepard, 1996). At the meeting just cited, one woman asked the consultant three times to provide examples of process language done well. The consultant politely refused, telling the woman to find examples from another newspaper he consulted for. Consultants are often seen as a barrier to mobility in that they redefine—or are perceived as redefining—the structures newsworkers have become accustomed to.

Moving between different properties in a chain as a means of upward mobility, even within the same company, is also difficult. If staff can find an open position, performance reviews are an influence. These reviews tend to be unflattering, even for good employees. According to many workers, performance reviews are tools used to justify keeping merit raises low. Setting improvement goals and highlighting successes (the formal purpose of performance reviews) are secondary to management's playing with the reviews' arbitrary numbers. In other words, giving a reporter three out of five points in a performance category like "Cultivates Sources" is difficult to oppose—especially considering that reporters must at times be adversarial with sources. The abrasive and forthright nature of some journalists, the difficulty many have with transitions, and the marginal nature of bargaining groups compound performance issues (an idea that is developed further in the next section).

In the modern newsroom, upward mobility exists most prominently in the realm of new digital products and the creation and utilization of nontraditional platforms, although this technical facet has little to do with journalism as a civic practice. Jane Singer (2003) has noted that online content is often the amalgamation of revenue-producing material from advertisers mixed with journalism intended as a public service. Online growth, as a goal, has a powerful influence on the decisions that managers make because they see it as an opportunity in the face shrinking revenue.

Because server management, information technology, and online product building are rarely within the traditional journalist's skill set, trained journalists more and more often work directly for online specialists. There has been much restructuring and adding of positions for those who are able to create, manage, and make profitable the digital world. Those newsworkers who cannot do these things or support them are often laid off.

Most of these sought-after digital specialists have little or no journalism background, but they often have good technical knowledge. Some clever newsworkers have found a place in this trend, but depending on the sophistication of the operation, they also find themselves practicing very little journalism in the traditional sense. Instead, they cultivate an assortment of materials, update websites, and report on online traffic. Moreover, they report to those who see journalistic value in terms of online performance.

For instance, a gallery has much more value than an investigative story because it generates many more hits on the website. Hits translate to dollars; thus, a photo gallery with 50 photographs may generate 50 page views from a committed viewer, whereas an investigative story, even one that spans several pages, will generate only a handful of clicks—maybe five. And these five views would mean that a reader had seen the entire story, through the end, but this is no guarantee in long-form journalism. In a gallery, each click of the mouse is a monetary success, and the labor required for this success is often as little as an afternoon's work. Investigative projects require a much more substantial time commitment; consequently, the gallery is more lucrative than the investigation. In this example, galleries generate 10 times the revenue that investigative articles do.

Market research has been prompting the redirection of resources for over 20 years; even so, newsworkers are often perplexed by the influence this research has on their superiors. Many newsworkers are put off by the conclusions for multiple reasons. Most prominently, they believe that such research infringes on core principals. Management tends to look at the digital paradigm as one more transition to which newsworkers will need to adapt, but there are few incentives in place encouraging newsworkers to try. Newsworkers have been the unwitting victims of online and digital products across the board, for they are asked to produce material outside that lies beyond their training. This material is often composed of frivolous, light journalism because such material is easy to produce or cultivate.

Even though news organizations are getting hits, these hits are not resulting in dollars. Online advertising is much less expensive to purchase than display advertising in print is, and therefore news organizations bring in lower ad revenues when they focus on online ads. One online specialist compared it to trading dollars for dimes, so news organizations are now trying to make as many dimes as possible. Those dimes and online hits do, however, demonstrate to management that traditional newsworkers can easily be replaced, given that the skills involved in digital work are learned in nonjournalistic disciplines, and younger newsworkers can easily be trained to do them.

Challenged Allegiance, Reorganization, and Control

Loyalty on both ends of the management-newsworker spectrum is strained as each side struggles to meet the other's needs. Seasoned newsworkers wrestle with the digital talent an employer wants and feel that the talents they have are not valued. Breed revealed that unions and bargaining groups have very little influence in terms of policy. This absence of negotiation between organizations and their workers allows organizations to make policy decisions with impunity.

Unions have influence only in terms of the contracts under which they operate and for jobs that are also clearly defined. Organizations learned long ago that a carefully planned reorganization could break apart many of the bonds of these contracts. Some unions have been traded away for a piece of the corporate pie in the form of 401(k) plans and profit-sharing incentives that management often refuses to put into place while dealing with unions. As organizations have become adept at manipulating structure, newsworkers often have seen their unions as toothless and have been happy to have a 401(k). These savings plans originated during more profitable times, but they were rarely fair. Organizations often refused to bargain in good faith by not sharing employee terms and salaries with the collective leadership.

In the newsrooms observed for this study, newsworkers were often stretched too thin to participate in union organizations. Still others felt that their participation would be detrimental to their upward movement. The Teamsters represent over 60,000 workers in the printing and publishing industries, many of which are newspaper print workers, delivery drivers, and designers (Teamsters, n.d.). The Newspaper Guild, Communication Workers of America, is a union of more than 34,000 journalists and media workers. It actively seeks members, works to improve the working conditions of media professionals, and promotes ethics and standards in the industry (Newspaper Guild, Communication Workers of America, 2012). The Newspaper Guild's website features news concerning labor issues and information about becoming part of the group, but it shows few direct ways for newsworkers to connect with one another, share advice, and mobilize workers experiencing common issues.

Of the newspapers observed for this study, only one was a union shop. One had no union at all, and at the third only an old collective bargaining agreement was in place. This agreement had last been updated in 2001, and only one member of the employee-representative board remained at the paper. The other members had been lost through layoffs and attrition. At properties that still maintained an active union, newsworker interests were perhaps more protected than at properties with no union affiliation, but there are many insidious ways to work around contracts. Management devotes a great deal of time and legal resources to that effort, ensuring that all legal requirements are met before proceeding with layoff directives. This forces union leadership to be reactive rather than proactive in advocating for employees. The following section represents a case in point.

Sidestepping

> *One executive editor found her photography department to be overstaffed. She had transferred from a larger newspaper, and that organization had maintained fewer photographers than her current post did. At the same time, the organization was redesigning the newspaper there and at several other sites. Leadership elected to create a more uniform and formulated template in page design. This was done so its flagship newspaper and other smaller newspaper properties could be designed by a single pagination team and work between products with greater efficiency.*
>
> *This directive for consistency was approached as necessary so that designers could manage many pages from many properties in a short amount of time.*
>
> *The placement of photos was constrained by this process because a set number and size were predetermined for the sake of consistency. Traditionally, designers use their discretion to place art and other elements on a news page. Beyond that, the redesign featured a "Local Focus" page that had only one consistent place for a photo. The plan was that this photo would be provided by reader contributions whenever possible, to encourage reader participation in the product.*
>
> *At the same time, management offered opportunities to photographers and others in the newsroom to cross-train with other areas of the operation, notably as broadcast videographers and online specialists. This was not framed as a job-saving directive in any way but, rather, as personally enhancing. The photographers who chose to defer cross-training picked up additional work so that their peers could participate.*

> Before any layoffs were announced, planning was well underway for a breaking-news team. The first skill mentioned on several of the job descriptions for this team was photography proficiency. These descriptions were not disclosed to staff. The breaking-news team was planned as a joint endeavor among several elements of the operation. Newspaper, online, broadcast, and radio would share the breaking-news team and its resources.
>
> The broadcast news director was clear that any new positions created were to be entry level with no previous union affiliation.
>
> Management decided on layoffs before the team's formation and justified ignoring seniority because not all the photographers had chosen to be cross-trained. Management informed union leadership that there would be photographer layoffs the week before they occurred. A Pulitzer Prize–winning photo editor resigned in protest before the layoffs could be made, and union representatives brought the situation to the attention of their lawyers.

This information attests a well-planned effort by management to trim older staff members with higher paychecks. The staff and union leadership certainly viewed the layoffs in that way. Organizations are perhaps not all as nefarious as this narrative indicates, however. The history of unions and the press has often revealed instances of management painted into a corner by union stipulations and contracts. These stipulations prohibited change and were technologically specific. Some newsworkers even had a job-for-life clause written into their contracts. Still, older newsworkers saw their younger counterparts unable to make what they considered a fair wage, and they believed this situation would not change.

The Pleasant Nature of Activities

In light of the previous sections, it may be surprising to learn that many newsworkers are fond of certain aspects of their jobs. Warren Breed explained that being among the first to know inside information and to deal with important timely issues was extremely attractive to newsworkers. In fact, this study confirms that those attracted to the news business appear to have an underlying need to see and understand the social mechanisms at work around them. The tasks associated with the job were, in fact, a joy when they aligned with the skills and core values individuals had entered the business to practice. Breed also observed that there is a sense of "in-groupness" in the newsroom. He noted that staff members were not treated as underlings but as peers, allowing morale to remain high and making up for relatively low pay.

This is no longer the case.

The appearance of in-group dynamics is still in place but is challenged by the organizational directives that force administrators to exercise a heavy hand (as evidenced by the earlier passage about Sally and Margot). In turn, there is little respect for executives or for any authority. Editors who are directly involved in the daily work and who have genuine empathy for those under them are often seen as comrades, but the same newsworkers who see some editors that way feel that they can see through the platitudes of other administrators. Morale is not high, usually because newsworkers do not see their goals aligning with those of the organization. At the same time, they are moved about the newsroom like chess pawns to protect the more important administrators in the back row. When administrators say they regret layoffs or are trying to avoid them, many newsworkers believe they are lying. When administrators say they will do what is best for the newspaper or the organization, newsworkers brace themselves for the worst. Moreover, this discord between newsworkers and administrators underscores the fact that newsworkers earn low pay and deadens the satisfaction of being part of a live wire organization. These elements remove the motivation for newsworkers to perform to their potential.

This communication deficit creates a quietly adversarial relationship between newsworkers and administrators, who both play a collegial game while conspiring to protect themselves. One line editor said of morale and the general tone of his workplace, "It's just not fun anymore, and this was not the case even a few years ago."

News Itself is a Value

Many managers rise from the newsworkers' ranks, presumably because the passions that led them to the industry in the first place philosophically align with those of the newsworkers they manage. Breed, addressing news as a value, concluded that news gathering as a goal trumps discussion about policy, ethics, and even objectivity. As seen earlier, it can also trump newsworkers' best interests in terms of job security. Breed noted, further, that executives and staffers are cemented together by their mutual interest in news. This promotes the in-group dynamics also noted earlier. After all, executives do not have time to chase down or present news stories.

Newsworkers often view their work as a higher calling of profound civic worth. This is a primary motivation for them; however, as financial issues, administrative concerns, and new technologies have challenged newsrooms, news as a core mission for administrators has become not only secondary but also poorly defined, as well. This is evidenced, again, in the experience of Sally and Margot. The question of what a news company's mission should be was once clear in the mind of the newsworker, but administrators now see a company bleeding money, and thus they seek more lucrative directions. This often leaves newsworkers asking *What do they want me to do?* and wondering, as Matt did, *How do I say yes to my organization?*

In meetings with staff, administrators still ask all the right questions, such as *Is it important? What does this mean? Is it civic-minded?* They also favor strong economic purpose in stories. The ability reach a broad audience is the definition of *impact* in news. This is often used to avoid conflict. Organizations favor stories about trends in part because of their broad appeal, but in fact these stories are a safe way for them to look at certain provocative issues. Writing a negative story about an individual advertiser or a large local corporation is specific and, as such, dangerous. Going after a trend, such as the use of public money for private development or dangerous working conditions, is safe. Administrators are held accountable to some degree for their decisions in the civic arena by their staff and by upper-level executives alike. These stories, broad in scope, lend themselves to the appearance of objectivity and seek to serve the largest number of people. But they also do a poor job holding accountable specific stakeholders, and many newsworkers consider this a disservice to the public.

Civic responsibility and a higher calling also serve a pragmatic function in the administrator's favor. This concern is a card often played when newsworkers broach the question of money. "If you're just in it for the money, this is not the profession for you," is a resounding theme among administrators, as if service and livelihood were exclusive. Many newsworkers report feelings of guilt and distaste regarding discussions about compensation, and those with the loudest voices in this area are labeled selfish or not committed to the profession. One veteran reporter said, "In the 30 years I have worked here, we have never been in a strong economic position when it comes time for my evaluation." The current economic challenges make the administrator's position even easier to argue for. Some newsworkers are so grateful to be working in the profession in this uncertain financial time that they are willing to overlook the poor raises; they feel sympathy for their administrators, and believe their hard work will pay off when finances even out. Staff members who expressed this opinion tended to be younger.

SEPARATION AS CONTROL

"Go work somewhere else" is the most heavy-handed form of social control in the newsroom. The example related in the earlier section

"Sidestepping" shows that newsroom administrators are actively looking for ways to streamline staff. Newsworkers see layoffs as part of their culture and as an inevitability of the profession—at least until a sustainable business model is achieved. As they are moved from position to position, many believe that if they do not say yes to these moves they will be replaced. They are often right. They have seen their colleagues laid off, many of whom had long tenures (nearly 30 years, in some cases), were loyal, and were extremely talented.

Money-saving initiatives have many incarnations, but the most lucrative come in the form of simply not paying employees. Layoffs, early retirement packages, and making the job so inhospitable that newsworkers move on are common practices. Once these employees have left, companies hire young, fresh, inexpensive workers, or they simply ask more of those who remain. These practices are observed, resented, and resisted by newsworkers, but few see alternatives. Furloughing employees is another money-saving practice that has been implemented at several newspapers owned by large corporations during the last few years.

Exploiting Furloughs

> *At one large metro newspaper, staff was told the financial situation was grim. For the paper to remain viable, management explained, unpaid furloughs would be required of each newsworker. This was a corporate-driven and companywide directive. Furloughs would consist of an unpaid week of vacation for all newsroom staff at every level.*
>
> *Losing a week of pay was challenging for many of the staff members. Those with savings were forced to dip into them, and those without were forced to pay bills with credit cards. They did this with the understanding that the company was in need and going through a difficult transition. The newsworkers believed that in the end, furloughs would save jobs. The hope was that this sacrifice would*

> give administrators time to refine plans and put them on more stable financial ground.
>
> The facts that each newsworker shared the burden and that it was stretched across each newsroom created a sense of solidarity in the community. Employees were rewarded when a companywide e-mail announced that the directive had paid off. At the end of the year, the furlough program had saved the company over $20 million.
>
> At the end of that year, the company CEO was rewarded with a $30 million bonus. One long-time respected and loyal investigative reporter was observed to say, "I couldn't pay my mortgage so he could get a $30 million bonus. From now on, I'm just doing the minimum—not a single thing more." Two large rounds of layoffs and many other individual layoffs resumed the following fiscal year.

My informant told me that the reporter quoted here could not in good conscience sustain his promise of a minimum level of work. But the damage had been done, and loyalty was affirmed as being a one-sided dynamic that poorly served the newsworkers' needs. Conditioned professionalism, practical needs, and civic responsibility in some ways overcame the sense of betrayal through corporate scheming, and newsworkers moved forward to the next day's labor. Most journalists take pride in their ability to watch society and to hold institutions accountable for their actions. They find naïveté counter to their mandate. Thus, when newsworkers are blindsided by corporate maneuvering, resentment amplifies, and trust is not easily earned again. Moreover, the tool journalists use to fight these injustices, the power of the press, is closed to them when dealing with their own corporations' behavior.

Layoffs are a precarious move for organizations to make, but as seen in the section "Sidestepping," organizations with active unions approach layoffs with careful legal consideration. In cases where no union is active, organizations can be much more cavalier in their actions, but layoffs must still be justified. For instance, a newsworker's being on a PIP (performance improvement plan), a written sanction issued to newsworkers not performing up to standards, is often reason enough to lay off a seasoned newsworker instead of a newsworker with a shorter tenure. As noted previously, the organization can eliminate unique positions (such as an assistant photo editor or a deputy features editor) without justifying it with a performance-related issue because the organization is eliminating the position, not the individual. The reality observed in this study is that those in unique positions had worked in the industry for a long time. And a longer tenure came with a higher salary. This set up an opportunity for legal age discrimination in the workplace—an opportunity that all the field sites in this study acted on.

Older newsworkers were often not given the opportunity to retrain for more stable positions in online departments, and there were several reasons for this. The first was that older newsworkers were more expensive, and eliminating their positions saved a great deal of money. The second reason was that older newsworkers were perceived by superiors as less technologically savvy than younger workers and were seen as unwilling to adapt to change. This dynamic also favored the organization in the following ways: Newsworkers who were seasoned were more likely to challenge directives, to point out inconsistencies with civic duty, and to remind leadership of past mistakes. Leadership enjoyed greater latitude with younger staff to define the organizational mission. In other words, eliminating these older workers also eliminated experience, confidence, and the tendency for workers to assert themselves.

One informant, a young woman, was moved from a copy desk position to the online desk immediately before a biting round of layoffs. She had been told behind closed doors that it would be wise to take the transfer. When I asked whether she was afraid of layoffs in the future, her comment revealed the ageism ingrained in the culture. "What's going to happen is going to happen, but I have two things going for me. I'm young, and I'm cheap." It is notable that this particular newsworker had no previous experience with online work, but she reported having been trained and feeling comfortable managing data in less than three weeks.

It is important to note that executives and administrators have the final authority in these moves; their judgment about a newsworker's value is final, and all these activities are legal, if not wholly ethical. The question is this: How does such behavior affect the newsworkers' understanding of their workplace? The way they do their jobs, in the long run, is affected by the dignity afforded or removed by their employers. How the industry will be affected by the loss of seasoned voices in the newsroom is another consideration. At the very least, the organization loses a source of long intuitional memory and community knowledge.

Employers do not remove newsworkers wholesale, and certainly there are many exceptions to the instances noted here. Many older individuals were visible over the tops of cubicles in the newsrooms I observed, but according to the newsworkers who informed this study, there were far fewer than there had been in years past—even just a few years earlier.

Newsworkers have long memories, and they are not a trusting group. They notice how their associates are treated. As colleagues, they lament the loss of co-workers, but as pragmatic workers, they also try to interpret layoffs in a way that might help them better understand what their superiors seek in their employees. It is often unclear to newsworkers, however, what missteps their colleagues had taken to warrant losing their jobs. Further, when the motivation for the layoff *is* clear, it often is received as fundamentally unfair.

PLANNING AND TIME MANAGEMENT AS CONTROL

Time is a difficult realm to navigate for the modern newsworker. Staff is cut to absolute minimums, often to the point that the use of time must be carefully monitored by management and newsworker alike. Organizations are legally required to pay newsworkers (many reporters and news presenters are paid hourly) for all of the time they spend doing their jobs. Some newsrooms have added time clocks to keep overtime under control. For Shelly, the features reporter and columnist at the small daily newspaper highlighted in the last chapter, this is an undignified cultural shift:

> *I always thought it was the strangest thing that reporters, who are asked to do a creative job, are paid by the hour and expected to create within a certain amount of time. I think a clock should never bind us.*
>
> *When reporters started being reporters, they didn't have to have a degree. You still don't have to have a degree, and there are no professional standards that would set us apart. [There is] no governing or licensing committee, so you are somehow not eligible to be salaried. I wish I were salaried because now that we have an actual time clock that we punch, if you spend five minutes laughing at something, you can't tack that time on at the end of the day.*
>
> *I always thought creativity shouldn't be abutted with a clock because sometimes you just don't have it in you between eight and five; you have it in you at seven or eleven. They don't want us to do anything on the road now. That's why it's so important that I come in on time —because I have to punch the clock. It's all about the clock.*

The control of movement has been somewhat justified by news organizations because many companies issue or subsidize mobile technology for their workers, allowing them to work on the road. Even so, reporters routinely clock out so that they have time to finish a project without going into overtime. Editors say this practice is unacceptable, but they have little inclination and take no action to monitor it. Reporters can easily reach sources by texting or e-mailing on the go. In 1999, fully 92% of journalists in the United States gathered news online (Garrison, 2001). The data needed for stories are often available online, reducing the amount of legwork required, even for some in-depth stories. The removal of travel time has, in many cases, increased reporters' productivity, decreased the need for staff, and kept employees on hand and in the office, subject to what many newsworkers see as the whims of editors. The reality is that editors can reach their workers through mobile devices whenever they wish, but many in the rank and file believe that editors are more likely to assess their needs differently if a reporter is not close by. Some reporters have found technology to be both a blessing and a curse in the control of their day.

The Art of Breaking News

> *Kelly was a breaking-news reporter at a large metro newspaper. Her day started from home at 4 a.m., and she was incredibly efficient. She began her shift while her children were still asleep, and from her home office she was able to check the police blotter and fire runs (all of which were available online).*
>
> *Kelly watched the local television news to make sure nothing had been missed overnight, she listened to the police scanner for breaking news, and she made breakfast for herself. On this day, Kelly was prolific. She Tweeted headlines as soon as information was confirmed by police, she called for details of an alleged rape case, and she gathered information for a story about the theft of $3,000 worth of brassieres from a Victoria's Secret store.*
>
> *Kelly had filed six stories online by 4:45 a.m., updated her professional Facebook and Twitter accounts, and informed editors of her work. After she filed the stories, she continued to monitor the broadcast news and her scanner, cleaned her kitchen, made her children's lunches, and got ready for the day. Her children were up by 7 a.m. Kelly carried her Blackberry for mobility and texted her editors with updates as she put her daughter's hair in pigtails. By 8 a.m., Kelly's children were off to day care, and she was on her way to the city building and jail to retrieve police reports and observe the arraignment of the alleged rapist.*
>
> *Kelly identified the rape case and the theft of brassieres as the stories of the day. She planned to visit the location where the alleged rape had occurred to conduct interviews before filing a longer story about it.*
>
> *This did not work as planned.*

> *She had hoped to avoid the office altogether because of the "depressing environment," she said. However, her editor called her in to the office to work on an unrelated story about the day's heat advisory.*
>
> *At the office she was asked not only to write the weather story but also to finish a colleague's story about a smoking ban and to update a missing-persons report from the previous week. Kelly filed a total of nine stories in less than six hours.*

Thanks to technology, Kelly was able to manage her time in a way she found beneficial. Internet, scanner, and smartphone technology allowed her to be remarkably efficient and to split her day so as to manage her personal and professional obligations. Nevertheless, there were some holes in the process that made her uncomfortable. She was not able to elaborate on the stories she had broken, and she found this to be a dangerous precedent. All of her information came from official reports, and no one edited her online copy. Although Kelly tried to be careful, she said that she was only human. In the race to be first—or at least, very fast—the editing comes later or not at all. Kelly said that this was not the fault of editors because they were shorthanded. Although the speed of her work may indicate that she was reactive to situations rather than proactive, Kelly was comfortable judging the importance of events that did not intrigue her and telling editors she did not plan on writing about them.

Technology and the realities of newspapers' financial situation have forced an environment in which more information must be seen as better information because depth is difficult to manage. Because space is limited in the print product, moreover, breaking news online has changed routines.

Communication as Social Control

Newsworkers are in the communication business, but they are the first to tell newcomers that they do not communicate very effectively with one another. This is an old adage in many newsrooms, but the reasons for poor communication are understandable in terms of a form of social control that is extremely beneficial to administrators. There are several levels of communication that newsworkers must overcome internally to determine what administrators and co-workers would like to see. It is the nature of human beings to engage and interpret one another's intentions, and this interpretation forms the core of social constructionist theory: Individuals must receive a message about their social self in order to interpret their social identity. Reliance on digital means of communication is the norm, as previously established, but what does that mean for newsworkers? Because editors see digital communication as an apparatus of simplification, they are increasingly comfortable asking for more work.

As observed by Tuchman (1972), the sheer number of stories produced makes newsworkers vulnerable to mistakes and to the internal judgments of superiors. Digital communication is not always a reliable means of clear messaging, but it is an effective means of redirecting work. Numerous times during this study it was observed that newsworkers, acting on text messages or short e-mails, would perform a function unsatisfactorily. This was because editors changed directives remotely, without regard to the stage a newsworker had reached in working on a specific task. Remote communication removes the respect for the labor that has been done. In doing so, it reduces tasks to the superficial label of finished or unfinished. Newsworkers not only believe their time has been wasted when things unfold in this way, but they also find that this phenomenon gives them less time to consider depth and attention to detail.

Although planning for these tasks usually originates with management, the redirection of work and its ramifications often reflect poorly on the newsworker. It appears to management that work is poor and that newsworkers manage their time inefficiently. The newsworker's frustration with this assessment is viewed as uncollegial. At the same time, management is also overtasked. This is perhaps the reason issues arise in the first place. Because managers are not involved in the nuances of information gathering and presentation, they misunderstand the realities of the work; thus, they abide few excuses for uncompleted work. All this gives management justifications for sanctions, poor performance reviews, and in-office labeling. This might take the form of "Newsworker X does not cope well with change, does not meet deadlines, and works poorly with management." These labels easily find their way into the cultural dynamic of newsrooms, and workers and management alike react to negative interoffice pigeonholing as though the label told the whole story of the newsworker's abilities.

Reduced staff and what one newsworker described as "kicking the can down the road" have further challenged communication. When one person in the course of a news shift cannot complete a task, it often falls to others to do so. This happens with the design of news pages, as well as in story production. Newsworkers do not generally like leaving work unfinished. They are concerned that it will not be completed properly. Leaving work undone challenges the newsworkers' sense of ownership of their work and creates concern that the uncompleted task will reflect poorly on them. The observations made for this study support this. Many newsworkers are so uncomfortable with unfinished work that they often clock out and complete the task at hand on unpaid time rather than leaving it for others to finish. One newsworker called this "kicking the can down the road." When newsworkers choose not to do this, those who must finish colleagues' tasks resent that this interferes with their own work and wonder why their predecessor could not finish—and resentment builds.

Challenged communication among peers takes other forms as well. Because the news cycle is tight, deadlines are relentless. Information producers struggle to get stories to presenters in a timely way. Informing them of changes is itself time consuming. Story budgets are rarely completed by the appointed times, and stories are often changed after deadline. Reporters and those on the gathering side of operations rarely experience negative ramifications from those on the presenting side of the newsroom when they fail to make their deadlines, whereas filing an imperfect story can result in uncomfortable sanctions to the reporter from management. Thus, for a reporter, it is better to be late than to be sloppy. This creates friction between gathering and presenting departments, but presenters must make do. They are forced to design what they describe as cookie-cutter pages (similar to those mentioned earlier, in Matt's story) and are forced to consider copy editing a novelty, so it is not always done.

A presenter's desk is a story's last stop before it goes to press, and that exacerbates pressures put on the individual. A missed deadline costs the company money in terms of printing and delivery labor, and it delays the product reaching the consumer. Because the news-production cycle itself is finite, there is also only a finite window during which consumers are willing to buy the day's news. The presentation newsworker internalizes tardiness as a personal failing that costs the company money. If the gathering newsworker misses a deadline getting work to presenters, however, there is no indication that he or she is burdened by such thoughts.

The presenter's desk is also where many digital tasks are addressed, such as uploading stories to the website. These added tasks, combined with gatherers missing deadlines, layoffs creating fewer editing layers between writer and reader, and the ever-present possibility of breaking news, frazzle and fatigue many news presenters. The situation drains them of their creativity and causes them to actively seek relief. This is normally accomplished by leaving the job (compounding the problem for others). The phenomenon is commonly called burnout.

To cope in this environment, newsworkers are often terse with co-workers and management alike. Some suffer in silence, and others resist pleasantries and carry resentment regarding the loss of co-workers, low wages, and long hours. Many are slow to forget past wrongs and fear that management is plotting against them. This, coupled with the dynamics already noted, gives management the impression that some newsworkers are socially backward. The result is social distance between these newsworkers and both their management and their peers, distance that further impedes communication and dissolves the collegial atmosphere that Breed cited as so attractive to newsworkers. Ultimately, distance between workers of all levels has become part of the culture, and the newsworker's individual talents, needs, and feelings have been marginalized.

This distance also allows management to become increasingly comfortable moving newsworkers to new positions, changing beats and duties, and ordering layoffs. All the while, newsworkers wonder where their autonomy has gone.

Research as Social Control

Organizational reliance on audience research also bears some responsibility for newsworkers' dissatisfaction. Individual organizations often do their own research, and newsworkers and editors are placed on teams to conduct focus groups and to gauge how the public will react to content and design decisions. As Underwood described in 1993, many organizational leaders see audience research as a service to readers. They have framed the research in this way so often over the years that it has almost become a core journalistic value. After all, putting the reader first is unselfish, and this appeals to the higher-calling and greater-good aspects of the journalism mystique.

Reality is somewhat different. Organizations are well aware which aspects of the operation cost the most money—printing and labor costs are the most prominent among them. Digital transition is the most promising area in which to alleviate concerns about the former, but according to industry experts, most operations still earn the bulk of their revenue from print advertising (Berte and De Bens, 2008). In contrast, labor can be pruned. As previously noted, organizations have drawn news presenters and resources together into design hubs where design desks produce news pages for many properties in the organization's chain. Many newsworkers are concerned that the individual personalities, traditions, and cultural variations of the individual communities served by each of these properties will not be reflected in the amalgamated design schemes. According to Underwood, "Newspaper content is geared to the results of readership surveys, and newsroom organization has been reshaped by newspaper managers whose commitment to the marketing ethic is hardly distinguishable from their vision of what journalism is" (p. xii). This profit-centered shift is veiled as a service to readership, but there are strong indications that results are predetermined by the perceived needs and desires of management.

Research Indicates What Readers Want ... But Only Our Research

> *Mitch, a presentation editor at a midsize metro newspaper, had many responsibilities, including running a converged presentation desk. Mitch was charged with learning what the best design scheme would be for merging the design and pagination operations of several properties.*
>
> *This effort would save the company money by decreasing staff and creating opportunities for the desk to manage outside design jobs. In pursuit of this goal, Mitch conducted focus groups with community members that featured prototype pages and surveys that gauged what was important to readers. The prototypes all had characteristics consistent with ease of design, featuring very little variation between properties.*

When I asked him which resources, previous research, and current trends he had incorporated into designing the prototypes, Mitch was at a loss. When a nonprofit consulting firm specializing in newspaper redesigns was mentioned, he understood the question better, saying, "They just want to be the experts and tell you what to do. We don't want to be told what to do."

Mitch explained that his research indicated that readers do not care about the individual "flavor" of a newspaper's design. This is a conclusion that directly corresponds with the goal of making all properties work under a single design desk. Mitch found that consistency had more utility than creativity did. Although Mitch's independent research contradicted conventional design theory, it did correspond to a cost-saving measure the company found favorable. Several designers in the newsroom noted that they had known all along that Mitch's findings would favor that measure because that was the administration's desired result.

In production and distribution areas specifically, there is an unprecedented movement toward cost saving. For example, one organization found in a research query that many women ages 25 to 45 prefer their local news in a more compact version than the one currently available as a printed newspaper. Some specifically called for a tabloid format. This study explains that the subjects represented "another voice" supporting ongoing research that calls for smaller, easier-to-handle newspapers. The study does not explain why this was tested, but the cost-saving implications are fairly obvious. This piece of research is unusual in that most of its results explore digital rather than print-driven opportunities among the demographic group. The implication is that this new information confirms an idea that was already being pursued. Although I was not privy to the specific questions and did not have access to past studies by the organization, the idea that research subjects volunteered, unprompted, that they would prefer a more compact newspaper is far-fetched. In other words, few would say they prefer a less easy-to-handle newspaper, and wrapping print implications into a digital survey is somewhat contrived.

This particular publication released plans to go to a 10.4 × 14.5 inch publication the following year, as opposed to a standard broadsheet newspaper. Production costs would reportedly fall to 25% to 30% of current costs, and the newsprint needed would be reduced by 33%. Although the publication promises that its content will not change in any way, it is difficult to understand how a newspaper can use 33% less newsprint and offer the same content. This is a leap in logic that has not been missed by newsworkers who are already struggling with trusting superiors. It is also notable that this organization is buying a press for this endeavor jointly, with a competing publication, and closing the production facility in its city. Newsworkers suspect more content will be digitally presented or abandoned all together.

Newsworkers see such moves as evidence that organizational directives do not support research but that, rather, research is conducted to support preconceived organizational directives. Because research indicates that a certain path may be lucrative, this justifies the organization's movement or its elimination of resources. This movement requires newsworkers to relearn tasks and adapt to new organizational needs. It also draws focus away from traditional civic duties. The same focus group that found a compact version of the newspaper favorable also indicated that women ages 25 to 45 wanted more watchdog reporting and local news, but this prompted no overt organizational directive. The research, which is turned into directives, generally supports what the company would find profitable rather than what favors journalistic values. Limited space in the print product has already led to breaking the routine news online. Car accidents, arrests, and event calendars are seen as adequate for reader needs. In short, these research directives are based, at least in part, on directions that management has already decided will be lucrative.

Conclusion

Friction can explode into frustration any time routines are disrupted, but organizational directives to follow policy are overt and common. As organizations try to find new effective business models, their attention is diverted away from newsworkers' needs and their performance. The desire to streamline and to handle more content in the digital realm keeps management from addressing low newsworker satisfaction and deficiencies in coverage. The current dynamic finds that it is not in management's best interest to value traditional tasks, like high-quality writing and photography.

Breaking news exists outside of meetings and often convoluted planning, but it adds one more component to a jammed news cycle. Speed is the order of the day, but depth is compromised. This is a dangerous game. Stories of a softer and shorter nature, typical of an online product, are considered safe in terms of libel and other legal issues, but the odds of libel increase with the speed of the operation. Add to this an organizational directive to see how many layers can be cut by laying off as many copy editors as possible, and newsrooms have a recipe for a lawsuit.

Organizations are not only in transition but also struggling to learn what they want from newsworkers. Organizations know they need a digital presence and have moved immense resources in that direction, but this has not proved lucrative. At the same time, newsworkers scramble to fill holes in the print product and to produce online content, all the while worrying about their jobs.

Those in management enjoy the isolation provided by the black ceiling, above which they can plan without newsworkers' interfering. This allows them to avoid lawsuits and to order directives before workers can react. It also cuts leadership off from valuable problem solvers and creative thinkers. Every indication is that management does not see this as a problem, given that managers have continually failed to reenergize their operations. Newsworkers do not see management's intentions, desires, motivations, or needs; thus, newsworkers are left guessing how they should behave, report on stories, and stay viable in their workplaces. Many times, sanctions result when good core journalism practices are at odds with organizational directives.

Research is executed with desired financial outcomes in mind, causing newsworkers to question the conclusions. Leaders are not trusted because their behavior seems to actively work against their own employees. This behavior is often intentional and overt and includes trying to remove union influence behind closed doors. More often, managers do not know the right answers and are pressured by corporate interests. In both cases, communication between newsworkers and management is strained, although neither group finds this favorable.

The result of all of these social controls is fear.

Chapter 6

Autonomy and Resistance

Organizational controls have taken on remarkable complexity in the wake of the digital paradigm and the monetary strain in the news industry. Management has become much more overt and committed to rebranding newsrooms as digital information centers rather than as newspapers.

As noted in the last chapter, administrators have many tools at their disposal for bringing newsworkers into line with these goals. At the same time, newsworkers have not abandoned their vocations as creative, civic-minded journalists. Although they understand the issues their organizations face, they are increasingly disenchanted with being treated as commodities and liabilities rather than as valued professionals. At least, that is the impression many journalists have with regard to the way their organizations view their contributions.

Journalistic autonomy is being challenged in newsrooms as never before.

Management, desperate to find an operational model that works, does not have time for discretion with newsworkers, and managers' sanctions are much more overt now than they were in the past. This chapter explores the ways organizations are perhaps poorly served by this behavior. Newsworkers resist unfavorable policy and challenge organizational rhetoric, especially when they see these behaviors as contrary to journalistic principles or as unjust to themselves or their peers. Because newsworkers form the front line of their organizations and are the last ones to touch content on its way to the public, they are positioned to resist. Practical concerns for their livelihoods and about organizational controls often lead to indirect resistance. The digital world, the source of much friction in the newsroom, has opened the door for newsworkers to exercise autonomy and to stay informed.

Practical Self-Directed Work and Social Connection

Reporters remain, at least on paper, extremely self-directed. Although assignment desks dispense work, this is often the result of the need for story quantity (for instance, there are not enough stories to fill a local section of the newspaper on a certain day), breaking news, or a request from management. These assignments may require a large swath of time, but the system does allow reporters the latitude to find and develop their own stories. In fact, it is expected that they do so. Even in cases when stories are assigned, it falls to reporters to choose the angle, sources, and style the work will take. This dynamic, like so many others, is challenged by the evolving needs of management. Given smaller staffs, administrators need to control and understand the information they will have up front so they can control their content. This was observed in the preceding chapter. But Breed pointed out that executives in his study could not be involved in the legwork of story building; thus, staffers were able to use their superior knowledge to subvert policy. This is still true, though to a far lesser degree.

Planning coverage before an event gives editors more control over the finished product but removes much of the organic spontaneity that reporters value. Work is in some ways much more controlled than it once

Autonomy and Resistance 103

was. Planning is certainly encouraged by executive editors as a virtue for staff to pursue. This directive could have easily found its way into the previous chapter, along with time clocks and mobile devices, but the idea of good planning often yields autonomy that favors the newsworkers.

The reality is that editors are stuck confronting a great deal of content. Although reporters have been laid off, the means to cultivate material for the paper have grown through citizen journalism, partnerships with other news organizations, and digital sources. Line editors have been laid off as well, forcing those who remain to contend with copy and to wrangle other material. Reporters are expected to write between two and three stories a day, and most line editors manage between six and ten staff members. Meetings, which could be vehicles for control, are often surface-level conversations in which general progress is reported. Getting all the stories edited is a challenge, and controlling the elements contained within them is nearly impossible. It is also not desirable.

Many line editors share core principles and empathy with the staff they manage. Autonomy itself is a principle for line editors that allows them to both manage staff and see to their own routines. Line editors have a role in the culture very different from that of upper management. They are on the front line with newsworkers and often find organizational directives as puzzling as many of their staffers do. They act as a buffer between management and staff, and though they must at times be the heavies and enforce policy, they have close connections to newsworkers (having often risen from their ranks). Line editors influence and change content, and they follow organizational directives, but they do not take action against newsworkers in a consistent way. They exercise their autonomy by allowing reporters to exercise theirs. For line editors, compressing tasks in the news cycle justifies letting go of some operational directives. This approach, along with the tradition of autonomy and the need to maintain collegial relationships with their staff members, lends to the self-guidance of the newsworker.

The close connections in newsrooms can have domestic considerations, as well. Several newsworkers observed in this study met their spouses on the job. Office romances were common at all the field sites in this study. Because partners were frequently promoted at an uneven rate, often a rank-and-file newsworker was married to a middle manager. One middle manager was married to a reporter who was also the vice president of the local union. Despite the fact that most organizations do not allow a spouse to supervise his or her partner, editors as a supervisory group must interact with each other. Thus, an editor supervising another editor's spouse must consider the social implications of communication regarding that partner. For instance, a meeting that includes criticism of an editor's spouse would be uncomfortable.

Peers were also involved in this dynamic. Job-performance issues, large and small, addressed or discussed by the offending newsworker's co-workers were wholly ignored when that worker's spouse was within earshot. The spouse of an editor is positioned such that negative rhetoric is curbed. Interestingly, this dynamic worked for both partners: the editor was defended in the newsworker's social circles, as well. This connection is a form of social protection and can give newsworkers added autonomy in their jobs, but it was observed to do little to defend against layoffs. Such connections also caused peer resentment.

Extranewsroom Resistance

Newsworkers have many outside interests beyond their work lives, and those worlds are not always entirely compatible with their organization's goals. Likewise, the organization also has goals beyond the confines of the newsroom. News organizations are members of a business community and as such must show civic responsibility and interest in the overall welfare of the communities in which they operate. They also must cultivate a presence in the community to remind readers of their brand. In general, newsroom staffs need not support these efforts

Autonomy and Resistance 105

beyond the specific tasks associated with their jobs, thereby giving newsworkers an opportunity to show dissatisfaction.

The United Way and Nonnews Tasks

> *Emmett worked as a copy editor and designer at a small daily newspaper. He considered his compensation modest, but he thoroughly enjoyed his work. Emmett felt that because the organization did not recognize him on what he considered an equitable financial level, there were limits to how the company should be able to engage him as an employee.*
>
> *One area of particular resentment for Emmett was the annual United Way fund drive. Once a year, within his paycheck envelope, he would find a donation form asking how much he was going to donate, on a per-paycheck basis, to the United Way. The amount requested was between $5 and $30.*
>
> *The week of the fund drive, there would be breaks in the day's routine during which employees were encouraged to play carnival-style games and participate in raffles and silent auctions. All this was to raise money for the United Way.*
>
> *Emmett found this extramedia influence insulting and considered charitable giving a private matter: "I can't buy a modest house or afford to leave town on vacation, but they expect me to give a portion of my paycheck back to them to give to the United Way. All so [the publisher] and [the company] can feel like big shits."*
>
> *Emmett would not in any way acknowledge the campaign, although e-mail, voice mail, and at times public pressure, urged him to do so. At the same time, he was certain that his work was above reproach. He said that invariably the publisher or the United Way committee chair would come to him seeking an explanation, to which he responded that he could not afford it.*
>
> *Emmett also did not play games on employee appreciation day, nor would he volunteer to work at the newspaper's information booth at the county fair or at business expos. He refused to play*

> on the company's softball team. Because Emmett was recognized as a consummate professional, his extraprofessional protests had little adverse effect on him, and he was always pleased that he could send these messages to the administration.

Emmett worked to resist obligations, preventing them from being placed upon him, and although administrators did not find this favorable, they had little direct recourse in sanctioning him. A United Way donation drive is clearly an organizational directive but is not related to the profession of news work. These non-news-related directives and tasks lie outside the publisher's ability to command. This is different from the ethics taboo Breed reported on whereby publishers would not overtly command that policy be followed. Publishers do make such explicit demands in the modern newsroom. However, giving to the United Way remains a nonbinding policy because it is beyond the executive's ability to legally enforce.

This is not a direct detriment to the bottom line, so publishers stand down, and the administrators who find this resistance unfavorable are normally high enough in the organization that several levels of administrators separate them and the newsworker doing the resisting (Emmett represents an exception in that he was contacted by administrators). Careful communication would need to be crafted to sanction a newsworker for not giving to a charity. In this instance, the message of dissatisfaction traveled up the ladder, and no direct feedback returned to the newsworker. Even though publishers can require newsworkers to work at a business expo booth, publishers must pay them. This is only an issue if they cannot generate enough volunteers (something that has reportedly happened).

Corporate giving is not always a noticeable area of resistance because newsworkers and corporations often give in some capacity for tax reasons. However, this giving—or lack thereof—is notable as another point of friction between newsworkers and administrators. When policy decisions extend beyond the newsworker's ability to participate, and when resistance to policy does not result in sanctions, newsworkers resist the policy to the organization's detriment.

How Newsworkers React to Big-Picture Decisions

One parent company gave a million dollars toward a development plan to beautify and add amenities to an urban waterway. This plan had been on the agenda of city officials for a considerable time. Some newsworkers were glad the company was helping beautify the city; others were shocked that it would do so during difficult economic times and in proximity to a number of layoffs. Still others were outraged that the company used funds in such an overt attempt to influence city policy (the proposed project cost $3 million and was not universally supported in the community). "Well, there goes your raise next year," one newsworker commented. Overall, this action caused divisive rhetoric and frustration. The general feeling was that the corporate office was lying about the company's financial health. On top of this, reporters were asked to write positive stories about the company's generosity, none of which would or could mention adverse opinions or the tax breaks the company would surely receive.

This is an example of what some newsworkers call *big-picture decisions*: choices made at a corporate level that come without warning and are not preceded by discussions with staff members. Big-picture decisions often have unanticipated ramifications and involve the attempt to ingratiate the company with employees or the community. In the example just mentioned, newsworkers were observed imagining ways to reflect this decision poorly in the publication. The most obvious way was to highlight how far the city needed to go to reach its goal of $3 million. Resisting the corporation is often subtle but is normally intentional.

Resisting amenities is another way newsworkers send messages of dissatisfaction to administrators. Amenities come in diverse forms: cafeterias, break rooms, onsite gyms, and gym memberships outside the facility. They may constitute group rates on cell-phone plans, allowances for certain equipment, or continuing education. Amenities may start at the corporate level or be site specific, but in both cases executives must try to extrapolate which employment packages will be most favorable and cost effective to the broadest range of employees. This works well at a macro level but becomes difficult to predict in individual newsrooms because newsworkers have been shown to house an assortment of values, interests, and personalities. Even the most loyal of employees will quietly resist when decision makers try to buy them with amenities, especially when they feel an ethical conflict.

Civic Duty beyond the Newsroom

> *A news operation began the process of consolidating its broadcast, radio, and print elements into one building. Barry, a line editor, had concerns.*
>
> *Barry was a native of the town in which he worked, had earned his journalism degree locally, and felt a great deal of loyalty to his organization. He aligned himself with most organizational directives and considered himself a company man.*
>
> *Barry was well respected by his staff and superiors alike. He was cautious not to participate in newsroom grousing, and even in the face of layoffs he kept his opinions to himself.*
>
> *Still, as a native of the city, Barry was concerned about the number of buildings being left vacant in the downtown area. He believed that the absence of a strong business presence in the downtown area would lead to urban decay and increased crime.*
>
> *The new facility his organization built to house all aspects of the company was located well away from downtown. It was able to hold the various entities that his organization required, as well as a new cafeteria with many different meal choices, a gym that staff could join for a small fee, and room for the business to grow as needed.*

Autonomy and Resistance

Barry agreed that the facility was better but was disturbed by the lack of responsibility the organization showed for the old building. The old presses could still be seen from the street through a window. The site was not repurposed in any way but sat empty for years as the trend Barry feared came about.

Crime in the area increased, more buildings sat vacant, and even the newspaper considered the city proper to be a secondary coverage concern. Barry promised himself that he would not buy in to the enticements promised with the new building. He did not use the gym or the cafeteria. Although he did not announce his reasons, he also did not keep them secret.

Barry normally eats lunch at one of several independent downtown businesses.

It is doubtful that Barry saw this behavior as resistance at all. There is little indication that resistance in the form of bucking organizational causes and amenities influences change in policy or day-to-day operations. However, such resistance does indicate that newsworkers feel the need to look for opportunities to reach administrators with their concerns. It further indicates that newsworkers will take action and resist in subtle ways when they feel challenged, repressed, or underappreciated. Given that these things happen on the periphery of the primary responsibilities and tasks involved in news work, they are tolerated by the organization.

News work is self-directed, and the will to resist exists in newsworkers, so the question becomes this: Can they resist when it comes to directives that more directly affect news work? In light of the social controls previously established, it would seem that they cannot, but technology and downsizing can advantage newsworkers as well as executives.

The Personal Brand

Historically, staffers who were considered stars by executives were able to sidestep policy much more effectively than younger newsworkers could. Now, even seasoned newsworkers face the ax as administrators look at cutting stars to save money. In spite of this, newsworkers have ways of building their value to an organization. A number of audience-engagement techniques exist in the digital world that newsworkers have started using on their own.

Many newsworkers, without prompting from their organizations, maintain Facebook and Twitter accounts. Also without prompting, they promote stories that appear or will appear in their print or online products. They build complex webs in social media of sources and often have large communities of followers. This presence is cultivated separately from the organization's efforts in the same social media arenas. The publications themselves, as well as peers of an individual newsworker, often follow their newsworkers on Twitter and repost tweets. Digital specialists representing the organization become "friends" with reporters and other newsworkers on Facebook and reply, along with the public, in their comment sections. Currently, organizations see this as advantageous, for it builds a synergy between media. However, no newsworker in this study said he or she felt pressure from employers to maintain a social media presence. Most organizations have digital specialists who formally perform social media functions for the organization.

This may sound like a new land of autonomous expression for newsworkers, but there are certainly limits to what the organization will tolerate in any public forum. The wholesale lambasting of the organization will certainly lead to a pink slip (if it is noticed). The real freedom of social media for journalists resides in other expressions, some of which have historically been taboo. A newsworker can, for instance, endorse his or her religion in a social media forum. Because social media is voluntary and personal, many organizations, including those in this study, have not introduced formal policy is this area. This is a somewhat different dynamic from what Epstein (1973) noted, discussing a ranking newsman who had never had a conversation with any peer about religion because he feared it would compromise his credibility.

The modern newsworker finds more freedom in the realm of personal expression. An individual can allude to a religious bias online and be associated with his or her organization without fear of reprisal. On Twitter one newsworker wrote, "What a fantastic service. Thank you Rev. [Name]. If you're looking for a great religious experience, visit the First Methodist Church this Sunday." This message appeared in a Tweeter feed alongside sources, editors, and story promotions.

Newsworkers may also exercise influence indirectly by pointing subscribers to something they themselves find interesting in a social media forum. This might be a comment made by a political pundit with a charged opinion or an article discussing the way another city is handling a problem similar to one the newsworker's own community is facing. Pointing to information is not considered taking a stance. Organizations at this point do not find this unfavorable.

As individual newsworkers build followings, the organizations that employ them gain online traffic with little risk to their objectivity or reputation. An organization's print product and directly associated digital products are held to another standard, but the convergence of digital worlds generates conversations regarding everything from politics and religion to sexual orientation and family life. Newsworkers use social media to promote civic organizations, hobbies they enjoy, and the work they do interchangeably. Doing so creates a picture of a richly human newsworker that resonates with readers and peers alike and cultivates an autonomous brand beyond that of the organization.

The Soft Organizational Directive

Organizational directives can be resisted through inaction in the hope either that the policies will blow over or that the organization is not wholly serious about them. Organizational directives are often not strongly enforced but contain loose ideas that are left for newsworkers to act upon. Organizations have adopted several ideas in the last few years that are associated with the digital world, but responsibilities and personnel associated with those tasks are often loosely defined. Creating video for an organization's website may, in one newsroom, be the responsibility of the reporter associated with the story; in another, it may fall to a photographer, as a visual journalist, to be the videographer. At still another organization, video may be the responsibility of a digital specialist. With a jammed news cycle, newsworkers are often given the latitude to choose which assignments they will give their full attention, whereas other assignments will be pushed down the road or treated only perfunctorily. In the case of photographers, video production for a website is a relatively new responsibility. Some enjoy the challenge, and others resent it, but video never replaces the need for photographs in the newspaper or on the website. With this in mind, photographers are able to justify covering only the basics of video production—or even not finding time for it at all.

Other photographers truly enjoy making video, almost to a fault. One photographer was observed editing and reediting a video piece until the task had consumed most of his workday. At the end of the shift, the piece was not done to his satisfaction, though it was extremely well polished and featured careful editing, B-roll, and music under the audio. It was so overproduced that the end product looked more like a promotion for the featured organization than a news story about it. In fact, the audience would need to work to find the news in the video at all. This seemed acceptable to the organization and the worker, perhaps because the industry tends to favor online products and perhaps because administrators see a polished product as having inherent value, without regard to news value.

Newsworkers are sometimes able to use this blind spot to build their own agendas and to drive their own workdays by presenting preferences that are most favorable to them as being most favorable to the product, all the while keeping alternatives quietly to themselves. One newsworker called this "driving the bus without being behind the wheel."

Adhering to Expected Tasks

Many newsworkers resist their organization by doing exactly what is expected of them. The ability to digitally retrieve information is not a new phenomenon, but often administrators have no idea what is available online. Reporters who prefer a gumshoe-journalism experience need only be ambiguous enough in their day's activities to leave the office. They can make rounds that feed their beats with information they find throughout the community or supplement that information as they wish with online data. This allows them to maintain the personal relationships needed to find good stories.

Most of the newsworkers observed for this study were diligent and hardworking. Most could be characterized as overworked. But there were a few exceptions.

Surprisingly, in light of the increasing complexity of the news world, in some cases minimal work was expected of newsworkers. This is certainly contingent on the day of the week, the specific tasks, and the organization's culture, but several newsworkers who were observed doing only the very basics of their jobs were still considered productive. This is yet another blind spot for executives, but the culture itself has been perpetuated by middle managers who also enjoy an easy workday. The root of this minimalist approach normally lies in an organizational culture that does not value its employees through monetary compensation, job security, or collegiality. Moreover, newsworkers remember a time when this was not so overtly the case, exacerbating the situation.

Some newsworkers have learned that the organization will take all the time and energy they have to give, but the same respect will not be returned to them, so they give the organization little of themselves. This may be understandable, but it causes friction with peers who are close to their work. These frustrations are reflected in Greta's comments, recorded in chapter 3.

Sunshine Blogs

Many executives depend on a code of silence among themselves and other stakeholders to keep sensitive decision-making plans from newsworkers while the details are finalized. This control has been called a black ceiling in this volume; the black ceiling may be opaque, but it is not impenetrable.

Many newsworkers are keen observers of their work environments, and although they are rarely given the complete picture of operational decisions, they are given enough information to recognize themes and trends that are unfolding above their heads. One way they are able to construct and predict the reality of their worlds, even without a complete picture, is through the anonymous independent blog. In the spirit of sunshine laws, which allow journalists to make government operations transparent, these "sunshine blogs" are set up so that newsworkers and interested parties can connect and make their companies more transparent.

Sunshine blogs are a relatively new clearinghouse for internal company information. In some cases it is not known exactly who contributes to a given site (certainly, this is by design) that spills information about company plans, but newsworkers find particular blogs to be remarkably accurate. They have predicted layoffs and executive changes at specific locations, added clarity to organizational directives, and peeled away the mystery surrounding certain acquisitions and policy. Many newsworkers contribute information to sunshine blogs. Information is compiled to create a more complete picture of events for newsworkers across chains, but more substantial contributors must exist above the black ceiling. Many newsworkers believe that contributors work in corporate offices or are themselves executives sympathetic to the problems newsworkers face in a changing industry. At the same time, many executives are not fans of these blogs, and some find them positively galling. They say these websites are not credible and have sanctioned newsworkers for looking at them on company time. With the demise of many collective bargaining units, these blogs act as a kind of labor community to address common concerns and grievances. The glee many newsworkers have experienced upon seeing their executives frustrated is certainly notable, as is a dynamic reminiscent of *The Scarlet Pimpernel*.

Forceful Personalities and News Judgment

The idea of "driving the bus without being behind the wheel" reveals another aspect of the dynamic in newsrooms. As previously observed, many newsworkers who have climbed the company ladder are those who are less ideologically opposed to organizational directives and corporate goals. Some would call them yes-men. Newsworkers characterize themselves and the personality attributes required to do their jobs as hard-nosed and abrasive (Mayer, 1987). Often, those attracted to the business are forceful and do not find brownnosing consonant with doing their jobs. This is consistent with the stereotype of the tough, no-nonsense reporter who will go to any lengths to get a story, all the while angering editors and infuriating sources. These attributes were not routinely observed in this study, but coarse behavior and routines exist in the culture nonetheless.

Given that norms, behaviors, and ethics were somewhat distinct from one newsroom to another and that individuals have been indoctrinated into the profession in different ways, conflicts arose. Newsworkers were often able to circumvent policy by citing precedents set by past decisions or by ignoring that which was not a formally stated rule. For instance, some newsrooms have a policy of keeping the names of minors who are the victims of violent crime anonymous. However, editors maintain the privilege of making that determination on a case-by-case basis. Perhaps circumstances arise in which a victim's credibility is called into question by authorities. In this case, editors may decide that it would be equitable to name the accuser. Down the road, newsworkers need not make a case regarding policy in this area. They have the autonomy to move forward as they please because similar circumstances have set a precedent, albeit an ambiguous one. The advantage in this case goes to the newsworker who initially chooses how to address the material in question. This is because from that point on, others must force a conflict or let the story go—the latter being the path of least resistance.

Even when such conflict is forced, often a newsworker with a forceful personality gets the desired result because policy is ambiguous. This dynamic also has a cumulative effect. If a newsworker has a reputation for being difficult, approaching him or her about news judgments or challenging him or her in other ways will be avoided. Often, a reputation for being difficult will keep coworkers and editors from approaching these newsworkers in the first place.

Conclusion

The deck is stacked against newsworkers in nearly every policy and personnel decision, but newsworkers are a resourceful group. Although the digital paradigm has closed many of the doors that made the traditional skills of news work desirable, it has also opened others. The autonomy of the Internet has allowed newsworkers to peek around the black ceiling above which executives plan policy changes that affect staff. Sunshine blogs have sprung up across the industry as a tool for understanding and controlling the newsworker's reality, monitoring corporate spin, and connecting with others who are trying to do likewise.

At the same time, pressures on administrators have forced them to look at big-picture decisions. This allows some staff the latitude to circumvent policy, exploit their administrators' ignorance of time requirements, and choose for themselves the tasks they wish to pursue. This is true of both digital and traditional tasks. This distraction within administration has also allowed newsworkers to build a hybrid personal and professional presence in social media.

Newsworkers experience little guilt in these activities. Loyalty is challenged because newsworkers have become keenly aware that their fealty is unlikely to be rewarded, and administrators are often working against them. The newsworkers' desire to resist is clear in their rhetoric each time the organization asks them to go the extra mile, buy into the organization's new projects, or give to their causes. Moreover, this behavior is not confined to a few disgruntled newsworkers but has burgeoned and become naturalized among many of the consummate professionals observed in this study.

Directives are challenged by those with forceful personalities and are relentlessly tested to determine how committed the organization is to those workers. It is also clear that neither side desires this adversarial relationship.

Chapter 7

Conclusion

The newsroom issues and dynamics highlighted in the preceding chapters contain the principal ideas reflected in interviews and observations, as well as in informal conversations, operational documents, and some shared organizational research. I would argue that these newsroom dynamics are representative of how social control and social construction manifest themselves in many newsrooms. Several issues deserve consideration here. One is the utility and practicality of traditional tasks as new media change ritual and routines in newsrooms. Another is the necessity of understanding digital influences on both the process of news work and newsworkers. The third is the way this new realm of newsworker reality could influence the future of news work.

De Botton (2014) has noted that media have replaced much of the function once served by religion in terms of guiding people's lives. Religion, as a metaphor, serves an understanding of operations, as well. Many newsworkers observed that the idea of journalism as a calling is necessary for the practice of news work, and it is in many ways as powerful as any organizational directive. This phenomenon springs from the investment journalists have made in the principles of civic duty associated with the profession. Education, history, the public good, watchdog functions, and the role of the Fourth Estate are the things journalists find sacred and the elements that make journalism credible in the eyes of the public. The belief is that journalism is more than a job, that it exists beyond capitalism, and that it is a benevolent practice.

According to Eric Rothenbuhler (1998), in terms of ritual, "the individual willfully submits to an external order of signs. We accept the command of ritual as if it were a material power against which we have none. In fact, it is not. It is an order of signs that has no power without our acceptance" (p. 129). If this is so, what is the reality of the newsworkers' world when they do not accept those signs from administrators? One overriding theme that emerged in this study is that whatever journalists have gained from digital technology—speed of news distribution and convenience in gathering information or contacting sources—they have lost in terms of comprehensive story content and meaningful civic work. When newsworkers are thrust into a world where their beliefs and core values are secondary, irreconcilable friction is created.

It is the Marxist view that in a capitalist society laborers are invariably alienated from the product, and thus they are separated from themselves (Marx & Engels, 1848/1998). The mistake made by media organizations is believing that journalism can be produced in the same fashion as manufactured goods. It cannot. Journalists are simply not laborers working in a media factory. In an industrial factory when there is a surplus of a certain component, a worker can be moved to the production of another component without compromising his or her values. This is not true of newsworkers. The informants in this study indicated that education, beliefs, and world views are intertwined with a passion for traditional journalism craft and a printed news product. Thus, one can argue that newsworkers cannot be removed effectively from that which they produce. Craft and newsworker are as indivisible as limb and body; the removal of the limb is possible—the body may still function—but the efficiency of the body is irredeemably compromised. This has been a point of friction associated with many technological changes and trends in the industry over the years (Hardt, 1990), but it is clearly seen as uniquely exigent now that newsworkers are in digital transition.

Technology is, at best, watering down the reasons many newsworkers went into the business in the first place; newsworkers want to practice writing (and other craft skills) just as a doctor practices medicine and, most important to newsworkers, to contribute to society overall as journalists answering a higher calling. Nerone and Barnhurst (2001) have argued that the loss of the journalists' gatekeeping function could replace "the benign dictatorship of the editor" with "the tyranny of the mouse." This study found a similar dynamic, but one driven by internal administrative directives. User-authored content was being actively solicited even as layoffs occurred. This was found result not from an external force but from a self-fulfilling trend designed to save money.

Digital products are not viewed by newsworkers in the same worshipful way the printed newspaper is. Having digital knowledge is certainly the number-one employment trend across journalism's landscape. Much as having background in political science, business, or sports is favorable with regard to certain beats, digital prowess is seen in much the same light in the field of new media. But it is platform-specific knowledge and as thin in civic function as it is broad in technological usefulness.

As Durkheim (1912/2008) noted, sacred objects have power, a power observable in the reverence a culture places on them. The physically printed newspaper has many sacred-object characteristics, and it is the physical manifestation of the individual newsworker's identity. As such, it has permanency and, at least to newsworkers, the power to change government, to protect the disenfranchised, and to inform the public. Editors carry it under their arm throughout the day like a weapon, and they pore over it like a love letter. Durkheim called the energy and reverence invested in a sacred object *manna*, and the stopping point for *manna* is the totem, or sacred object. It is not unreasonable to see the physical newspaper in the role of a totem. Journalists devote their creative energy, professional ethics, and personal character to this very public and social object. They interact with it intimately, labor over every decision, and take personally every mistake associated with it. Newsworkers await the public's acknowledgment as they interact with the newspaper, and many believe the smallest decisions regarding those printed pages can bear profound consequences for democracy and the Fourth Estate. They hold tight to the society-changing "miracles" of the past, such as Watergate and the civil rights movement, all the while looking for the stories that will lead to the next validation of their faith.

Many scholars have asserted that the digital transition has obscured what a journalist truly is (Allan, 2006; Kopper, Kolthoff, & Czepek, 2000; Singer, 2003). Given that the loss of autonomy is technological in origin, newsworkers try to draw the line at letting that extend into their civic-mindedness. Sometimes they succeed, but more often they fail. One thing is certain: when the civic nature of the profession is removed from journalism, the newsworker's passion for the job is also removed. Older newsworkers see this clearly, and organizations have been slowly removing older employees from their newsrooms in favor of those who are more digitally savvy, cheaper to employ, and less likely to question organizational directives. Even when older workers are retained, they are often wedged into positions for which they are not trained, destroying their confidence in their work as the organization destroys the positions that many of these employees spent years cultivating. This renders jobs in the newsroom unsatisfying and disheartening.

Civic principles have power, just as news itself is considered a value. Often a newsworker's values have the power to hold them in positions they do not find entirely palatable. This is another point of friction within the culture. The history, traditional tasks, and even the sacred focal points that Rothenbuhler might call the voluntary performance are no longer valued by the organization—at least, not in a way that newsworkers can see. Rothenbuhler, like Paul Hirsch (2000), found that those things which are symbolically meaningful affect the roles individuals perform. This idea can naturally be extended to newsroom crafts. These performances, once touted as appropriately patterned behaviors when it benefited the organization, have been diluted by economic stresses and desperation for audiences.

A newsworker's time is distributed so that watchdog functions and traditional crafts like writing and photography, which attracted many newsworkers to the business, are given only a passing nod in favor of updating a website or a calendar item. This makes the function of journalism a trivial social construction and renders the rituals surrounding them profane. The rituals related to digital journalism do not have the same symbolic effect on the serious life, as described by Rothenbuhler, as does print journalism.

This makes digital journalism endeavors profane rather than sacred.

The platform itself has no physical permanency. The digital world by its very nature is nonsubstantive, and its rituals lack the traditional meanings and focal points a print product contains. In this case, a digital product does not fit Durkheim's definition of a totem in the way that a printed newspaper does. The digital product lacks a physical and permanent stopping point for the newsworkers' *manna*, required for an object to be sacred. Moreover, digital news is not consistent with Rothenbuhler's definition of ritual because it is not voluntary. Organizations have taken a hard-line approach to digital products in an attempt to force newsworkers to see them as new core values. Thus, statements like "We are no longer a newspaper; we are an information center"—an overriding organizational directive—justify cutting news staff to the bare minimum.

The pressures created by changing platforms and economic stresses have forced organizations to reconstruct the world of newsworkers' values. They do this by issuing multiple organizational directives and framing them as reader-centric services. To continue the religious metaphor, this is as popular among newsworkers as demanding that they worship in a church not of their choosing would be.

According to Underwood, people have not responded to market-oriented journalism. Organizations look to research for answers about a broken business model but rarely look to the newsworkers who confront readers and the community every day. Further, members of management change the organization only on their own terms. This study indicates that newsworkers themselves do not find market-oriented research particularly effective, and resisting it is ingrained in much of newsroom culture. The few newsworkers who have been invited to become involved in the process are challenged because they suspect or are overtly told what the organization would like to see as conclusions. Eventually, these conclusions manifest in newsroom routines, but they are never naturalized by newsworkers at large, so they do not become rituals. They become what Schlesinger called a *novelty of change*, or a change with little substance or permanency. What has become a naturalized ritual in the newsroom is the need to resist these directives.

Newsroom rituals and routines are necessary if goals are to be achieved and social order maintained, but newsworkers rage against the prescribed order, and they do this at a level of influence central to the operation, at the core of Shoemaker and Reese's (1996) hierarchy of influence. Newsworkers are the first and last to touch the material that builds the organization. Logic dictates that this position would command a healthy respect from executives, but the latter rarely demonstrate such esteem and do not appear concerned about possible consequences.

Although newsworkers experience autonomy, they do not have adequate knowledge about the values and goals of decision makers. If clarity exists above the black ceiling in the realm of management decisions, that clarity rarely extends below it.

There are mixed messages and double dealings in the way organizations contend with newsworkers. So foggy are management's goals

Conclusion 125

and intentions that many newsworkers have concluded management simply does not have a plan. Organizations tell newsworkers that they are valued for their traditional skills in one breath and lay them off in the next, all the while moving younger newsworkers into safer digital jobs. As executives deal with newsworkers, they voice support for traditional crafts and core values when it benefits the organization, and they frame those beliefs as dated when they do not match monetary objectives. As Antonio Gramsci (1940/2000) noted, the media are constant sites of struggle between hegemonic and counterhegemonic ideas. This remains the case in the modern newsroom, but it is a perpetual battle for administrators to achieve enough consensus among the work force for things to operate smoothly. That consensus is never truly achieved, and things rarely operate smoothly. Consensus in the modern newsroom often gives way to overt demands as the organization's very existence is threatened, or at least perceived to be. Any consensus-like dynamics are clearly framed as a courtesy extended to the newsworker from the organization.

Newsworkers have long memories for history, institutional knowledge, and what they consider poor leadership. The current newsroom model calls for light engagement with both work and readers. Consumers, through online traffic, influence news judgment a great deal. This traffic often determines an organization's content decisions. This very fluid relationship is favored by organizations, at least until they can find firmer ground on which to build a new business model. Meanwhile, the news that these organizations present remains soft, and readers have little ability or motivation to retain it.

As conditions change, they make transparent the function and reality of the individual's place in an organization. Media organizations introduce directives to control the social and professional values inherent in newsroom culture, and the more desperate they become to remain financially viable, the more transparent their controls grow. As newsworkers experience this, they resist in interesting ways. Some resistance is effective, but most is not. This may sound like a victory for organizational control, but the matter is not that simple. Journalism does not exist in a static state. It is a linear endeavor that takes place in a perpetual cycle of decisions and countless human choices. Journalists are uniquely positioned to make those continual choices in relation to one another and to their products. Social construction is a result of those choices. Social constructionist dynamics in the modern newsroom can be pointed and specific, but they are not permanent and fixed for all time. It is the newsworkers' ongoing choices that carry the most profound influence.

Some newsrooms are sad places with more empty chairs than occupied cubicles. Some organizations have gone so far to as to reallocate space as meeting areas, common areas, or break areas, as though the newsworkers who once filled those places never existed. As one reporter pointed out, "Sitting on a couch for a meeting is a poor substitute for job security." Newsworkers are invariably confused. Several years ago, companies reported record profits but continued to lay off workers (Stucke & Grunes, 2009). In 2011 and 2012, during this study, organizations were by all accounts still making money but not with the very large profit margins they once did. Most newsworkers think their companies have successfully created a culture that perpetuates the myth that they are always experiencing difficult financial times.

Another means of control that organizations use to minimize newsworkers' pay is civic function itself. The idea that the higher calling of journalism and the goal of serving society's needs outweigh monetary considerations is still perpetuated in newsrooms, although executives cite money as the basis for nearly every decision they make. Thus, the latitude organizations have to demand journalistic professionalism is in opposition to their behavior in terms of capital. There has, in the mind of many newsworkers, always been enough profit for companies to offer employees compensation comparable to that earned by people of similar education working in other fields. One newsworker indicated that executives do not value "soft skills"—the skills that do not directly generate wealth (reporting, writing, editing, etc.).

The problem is compounded and justified by a poor economy.

For instance, there is little evidence that such newsworker tasks as editing, done well or poorly, will lead directly to profit—at least, no such evidence exists in the recognized social contract between newsworkers and administrators. This, along with the layoffs of friends and the difficulty of tasks, has turned once-vibrant newsrooms into shadows and has destroyed morale.

One trend that has restored some level of this lost morale is convergence. Different media working together must cooperate and communicate in order to understand that with which they are not familiar. The communication involved in managing different media has led to energizing conversations regarding coverage priorities and how to best serve the community. As those newsworkers who practice the craft in broadcast, radio, and print work together more, they must find a common cultural language beyond their respective media. This language is often that of journalism and service. Online publication, as a unique media outlet, does not share in this dynamic. Practitioners in other media see Web endeavors as an obligation and an ethereal land of fuzzy goals. This is often a point of frustration for converged media outlets as newsworkers and managers try to decide whose responsibility online activities will become. Neither newsworkers nor administrations want that responsibility; thus, the digital specialist gains more power. Newsworkers are still expected to do traditional tasks and see the digital world as a burden, and administrators and newsworkers both resent and appreciate digital specialists for taking it off their hands.

Adversarial behaviors arise between executives and newsworkers almost every day. They damage the cooperative function, which Pierre Bourdieu (1984) called *social capital* (the positive outcomes of social relations), and force distance between the employer and the employee

—destroying the patron-client dynamic that once existed and upheld journalism as a common goal. Control often exists in the preselection of right-thinking people, and many are willing to put the company before civic responsibility. In the modern newsroom, right thinking also extends to those who are digitally savvy. However, members of leadership are often as clueless about the digital realm as older newsroom staff members are; thus, their motivations are no longer simply to hire yes-men but to hire those who will remove the scary digital ghost from their line of sight.

The damaged business model has changed relationships and moved those in the press away from collegiality (Schlesinger, 1999). This investigation explores how executives have exploited the distance between themselves and newsworkers in a number of ways, but they are not the only ones exploiting this distance. In the face of change, some individual newsworkers have found routines in which to hide. As the streamlining of work has made many traditional tasks more efficient, some newsworkers have not absorbed additional tasks in order to make their newsrooms more successful. Photographers no longer have darkroom responsibilities, and reporters have many resources at their fingertips online, but in some cases, those surplus minutes have not been turned into a fuller expression of their craft. This happens in part because of laziness and owing to the sentiment that the companies are getting what they pay for, but in most cases the dynamic is more complicated.

Newsworkers see the streamlining of their jobs through technology or other means as equalizing. In other words, they felt overtasked in the first place, and technology or the reallocation of tasks makes the job more reasonable. These men and women have a full understanding of why they chose news work and often feel little responsibility for other areas in the newsroom that do not involve their personal skills. In operation, a photographer who finishes his work an hour early is unlikely to willingly help an overwhelmed copy editor design pages, look at page proofs, and enter community calendar items. More likely, the photogra-

Conclusion 129

pher will relax, read e-mail messages, visit with co-workers, or simply leave for the day. This was true of many newsroom positions observed for this study.

Administrators are also responsible for this dynamic to some extent. They do not wholly understand the responsibilities and functions of every member of their team. They adhere to old job descriptions or have constructed in their minds a false idea about contributions. A wrong understanding of newsworkers' tasks among administrators is perhaps one of the most prominent findings of this study, and this misunderstanding normally hurts organizations and newsworkers alike.

The newsrooms studied for this project were struggling economically, and that struggle led to challenges in core values, treatment of newsworkers, autonomy, and creativity. Naturalized aspects of the culture have exacerbated these problems, as has the loss of collective bargaining power. These newsrooms are filled with skilled journalists with many years of experience, all of whom were trying to serve readers and present people with the news they need to exercise good citizenship. Many older newsworkers with extensive community or institutional knowledge had been laid off or felt undervalued. Administrators often took an adversarial approach with their staff. This management style, combined with newsworkers' fear of layoffs, kept newsworkers from doing what they considered their best work. Instead, their work was geared toward what would be acceptable and safe in the eyes of the organization.

Hegemony is evident in the organizational decisions of newsrooms every day and culturally enforces the rituals, routines, and values that keep managers in their positions. This control has created no observable positive changes for newsworkers or their craft. In the end, organizations are not serving themselves with this practice. They are destroying the passion newsworkers have for their jobs and creating incentives for them to leave the industry.

The newsworker's world is defined by dominant administrative views, and organizations are attempting to re-create the reality of journalism's core values by privileging digital work. This emphasis on the medium rather than the message obscures good journalism by marginalizing the newsworker. These issues are augmented by poor organizational research, which is distorted by economic stress. As a result, the insights of newsworkers are routinely ignored. Moreover, as organizations disenfranchise newsworkers, the communities they serve suffer because few know the issues, challenges, sources, and flavor of a community as well as the newsworkers who live there.

STUDY LIMITATIONS

This study set out to produce a broad understanding of the modern newsroom by examining the culture of three newspapers. The idea was to spend time observing their operations so as to better understand how new digital technologies, old routines, and civic responsibility metamorphose in an industry that is economically challenged and in transition. A great deal of effort was made to situate news practices within the broader frameworks of social theory, but it is important remember that this is a micro study of only three daily newspapers in a country that is home to more than 1,400.

In a study such as this, the standpoint of the researcher must be acknowledged. In participant observation, the researcher is in some respect the measurement tool. The questions asked and my positioning in the newsroom, as well as my prior experience in similar environments, have become an indivisible part of the study. I am not only a researcher but also a former journalist and editor with 11 years of experience. Having spent 6 years outside the industry, I was surprised by many of the changes I found upon returning. These surprises and status quo experiences were instrumental in shaping the data collected and the analysis.

Conclusion 131

As a former newsworker studying newsworkers, I was in the midst of people like me. This background helped me gain entry to sites and provided knowledge of industry jargon and work-related pressures. It also allowed for rapport to be developed quickly. Although I was extremely open with those I was working among about the goals of this study, often newsworkers and administrators felt a causal notion that this research was geared toward the mechanics of newsroom operation and not likely to be critical. Even though mechanics in newsrooms have changed in recent years and understanding them is fundamental to understanding the newsroom routines and culture, there is much evidence of dysfunction.

Time with any given newsworker was limited, and that certainly had an influence on the data collected, but the newsworkers involved in this project were extremely candid. In many cases, that someone was inquiring about their work was refreshing for them. And this inquiry was perceived as therapeutic, giving newsworkers an opportunity to share thoughts and feelings they had long refrained from expressing.

This study was newsworker-centric. Though I interacted with and interviewed administrators at various levels, this research is attuned to the cultural reality of the rank-and-file newsworker's world. Pressures and influences exerted on high-level administrators certainly carry their own challenges, but this study visits these influences only in tertiary ways. Executives were not the focus of observation, and the reasons their behavior manifests as it does were beyond the scope of this study, though they are wholly influential to the newsworker's world.

I was also the tool for the selection process. The staff members selected for participation represent as many variations of newspaper newsworkers as possible. This group of sources showed interest in the study and were receptive to my request to shadow them. Had different individuals been selected, the conclusions might have been slightly different. This research tends to highlight problems; often, the positive and fulfilling elements of news work have found only a minor voice in this study. They were certainly present but were far from dominant themes. The related issues and consensus voiced by newsworkers in different jobs and newsrooms provide convincing evidence of the validity of the findings.

FUTURE RESEARCH

This project raises many questions about newsroom culture. A few areas that should be addressed in the future related to the pressures and influences that occur in the world of news administrators and executives. This study identifies a black ceiling above which these key players operate. Rank-and-file newsworkers are not privy to this world or to organizational directives, and the seemingly strange conclusions stemming from organizational research often dumbfound them. Given the transition news organizations are going through in terms of digital products and an evolving business model, the question of how these variables will resolve themselves is paramount to sustaining an understanding of cultural reality in newsrooms. In addition, how might the dynamics observed in this research compare with those at broadcast or radio operations? It has been strongly suggested throughout this study that the structures and systems at work in a for-profit newsroom heavily influence its culture. A study at a nonprofit news organization, such as ProPublica, would be valuable for understanding how and whether journalism and newsworkers may be engaged under a different model.

Given the lack of control newsworkers feel in their own environments, exploring ways to amalgamate the autonomy they once enjoyed with digital and evolving platforms is another direction for future research. Are there better models for organizational structure than the dominant capitalist, corporate, growth-oriented models that have recently served newsworkers and the civic function of journalism so poorly? Because newsworkers represent the front line in public understanding of the breadth of issues that affect their lives, any research that facilitates a deeper understanding of their world would be welcome.

Appendix

Detailed Methodology

The social construction of reality has many interpretations, but it also has enormous potential for describing the reality of the modern newsroom. Potential influences on newsworkers are plentiful, but little research reveals a consistent pattern of what newsworkers themselves find influential or of what they might choose to prioritize. With this in mind, I needed a vehicle to explore how newsworker dynamics are internalized and acted upon by journalists in order to gain a deeper understanding of their reality.

As I considered these research questions, along with literature on the social construction of reality related to mass communication, I settled upon an amalgamation of several qualitative research methods as optimal for this project. Because this research was conducted in the natural world, and given that the complexity of work relationships, attitudes, and job routines are germane to understanding changing newsrooms, a qualitative approach was chosen to allow me the latitude to be responsive and observant in a busy newsroom environment often rife with sensory chaos.

This work was conducted in two phases. The first comprised a series of face-to-face interviews with journalists in order to gain an overview of their concerns and their observations of the fields in which they were working. The second phase was a period of participant observation exploring the ways these concerns played out in the field. All told, data were gathered from more than three months of observations, from 31 formally shadowed informants, and from 45 informal informants met at the newspapers while conducting the research. Thirty in-depth interviews with newsworkers and administrators were conducted over the course of the project (25 in phase 1 and 5 more in phase 2), and assorted internal documents, such as news budgets and employee handbooks, were used when accessible and pertinent. The literature cited in the study provided a map for highlighting newsworker studies and social constructions of reality. This literature was used to inform my presentation of how the industry has evolved over time and to justify the need for further study. The two phases build on each other and add to previous studies of newsroom dynamics.

PHASE 1: INTERVIEWS

In the first phase of this project, results of an analysis of 25 in-person interviews with journalists were compiled from midwestern daily newspapers with circulations ranging from 8,000 to 160,000. The subjects interviewed were front-line newsworkers, defined for this study as nonmanagement or first-tier management employees who produce or process news and editorial content for print or online consumption. This included reporters, copy editors, photographers, designers, news-service workers, and line editors (editors who directly supervise the workers in the preceding list). The reason for selecting lower-echelon journalists over higher-ranking management was to limit the influence of organizational concerns, given that this study sought the most honest feeling possible rather than a company line.

This approach privileged individual issues, examined the hierarchy-of-influence model through a lower-echelon lens, and allowed interviewees' perspectives to be examined without management's making newsworker voices indistinct. Because this analyzed feelings, motives, and behavior—and centered on key questions—structured interviews were chosen as the methodology. Interviews proved to be an extremely flexible method for gathering data, yielding information I had not planned for or anticipated. According to Leedy and Ormond (2001), interviews can reveal the conscious reasons for actions and feelings, as well as people's beliefs about the facts.

Another important concern was the accessibility of newsworkers for candid and honest interviews. To further this goal, the journalists were granted anonymity, and I promised that they would be identified only by a pseudonym and demographic information when necessary. Furthermore, the specific publications where they worked have been held in confidence. All interviews with newsworkers were conducted face-to-face, in private, in empty conference rooms at their workplaces or at an offsite location, such as a coffee shop or restaurant. All interviews were recorded, and transcripts were made from those recordings for analysis. Beyond the criteria already noted, journalists were selected for this study based on their willingness to participate and to answer all the questions posed in great depth. Informant newsworkers were approached for this study through e-mail messages and telephone calls to their respective organizations or via social media. When they were told the study involved giving a voice to newsworkers in a changing newsroom culture, they were often eager to voice their opinions.

Given that only 25 journalists were interviewed, the first phase certainly does not represent all newsworkers in comparable positions and publications. Rather, it yielded ideas from which themes could be extrapolated and revealed remarkably similar themes that allowed focused observations in the next phase. The interview questions were not disclosed to participants before interviews in an effort to evoke spontaneity and genuine responses. Prior to each interview, participants were told they would be asked about their feelings regarding newsroom culture. Each interview included the same six questions but allowed informants to guide the direction of the discussion and to be as conversational as possible. This drew out similar themes, though often in response to different questions, and follow-up questions encouraged informants to elaborate on ideas. The questions, developed from social construction theory and newsworker literature, were designed to be ambiguous enough that subjects would freely associate issues that concerned them. The goal was that the themes identified would inform the participant-observation phase of the study and allow a comparison of attitudes toward practice.

Because informants were encouraged to guide the interviews, the duration of each interview varied. The longest interview was 36.13 minutes; the shortest was 7.44 minutes. The mean (average) of all the interviews was 18.31 minutes, and the median was 19.28 minutes. In all, the data were compiled from 7.08 hours of interviews. This does not include the informal conversations, which often revealed intriguing and useful information; these were recorded in notes but not audio recorded.

This stage of the study yielded several themes that became focal points for the observations in the next phase. These themes were cynicism and distrust as cultural values, the perception that newsworkers are neglecting civic and professional functions owing to increased responsibilities, the perception that management favors digital competence over traditional skills (such as writing, photography, and editing), and a keen awareness of organizational controls. These themes were observed in the participant-observation phase and have been engaged in the text through the work of other scholars and through interviews conducted for this study. The interviews also revealed that newsworkers were aware of a loss of ideological control in the newsroom and that they felt powerless to change this situation. Furthermore, organizational influences were perhaps more transparent because of the training and nature of journalism work. The biggest restriction in the interview phase that needed to be considered before the study progressed was that many individual journalists were not consciously aware of the influences imposed upon them. Thus, further observation (phase 2) needed to test the assertions made in the exploratory interview phase.

Appendix 139

PHASE 2: PARTICIPANT OBSERVATION

Armed with the results of phase 1, I observed three daily newsrooms as field sites. The newsrooms differed in size, ownership, and structure but were similarly geographically located. The goal was to determine how newsworkers interact with the themes that surfaced in phase 1. The newspapers were chosen with the aforementioned characteristics in mind but needed to meet other criteria as well. Management and staff needed to be willing to allow a researcher into their newsroom operations, and locations needed to be geographically close so that travel from site to site on a weekly basis would be feasible.

Newspaper field sites were observed from June 20 to October 20, 2011. The circulation at the newspapers varied from more than 150,000 to less than 13,000. One newspaper had a union affiliated with a national guild that covered its editorial workers; another had no union, but a collective bargaining agreement was in place (it had lapsed but was still legally binding); and the last newspaper had no union affiliation at all. Ideally, three different companies would have owned the three different newspapers. However, not all the newspapers that were approached because they met the inclusion criteria were willing to accommodate observational research in their newsrooms. The same large media corporation owned two of the newspapers, and a large nonpublic media group owned the third. All these newspapers were located within 150 miles of one another. Again, this was necessary in order to eliminate proximity as a variable and to allow me to observe all three newspapers during the same period. The news managers and editors who granted me permission to observe their operations requested that the publications not be mentioned by name. This term was readily agreed to, given that anonymity was desirable to protect the newsworkers who were observed. Anonymity also promotes candor and is in keeping with ethnographic tradition.

I spent one to two days per week at each site for a period of three months, observing during standard work shifts (about eight hours), using the ethnographic tradition of participant observation. Field notes were taken within each newsroom as I participated with and observed newsworkers performing their jobs. The participant aspect of this study varied from site to site. Members of management were encouraged to use me as needed to perform newsroom work, but none felt this was appropriate. I am an experienced journalist, but the reasons given for not putting me to work included discomfort with work being done without compensation and not having time to train a newcomer in their specific operation (time shortages, ironically, that had resulted from dramatic staff reductions). Therefore, I essentially engaged in job shadowing to gather information, helping the newsworkers whenever possible, and learning the specifics of their various jobs. The only activity outside this interaction occurred when I led a training session with several editors in pagination software.

Don Heider's book *White News* (2000) utilizes similar ethnographic methods, and that study was performed in a similar media environment. Heider situated himself in two broadcast newsrooms for five weeks each in order to study the internal reasons why there was less news or more negative news involving minorities than involving other groups. Like me, Heider is the product of the discipline he wished to observe (he is a broadcast journalist; I am a former newspaper journalist); he too spent several years away from the business doing extensive reading, thinking, and writing about the news practice before returning to conduct his research. His understanding of the culture allowed him to quickly acclimate to the environment and to achieve informative rapport. This proved true in my own study as well. I attended news meetings, interacted with newsworkers, and accompanied reporters and photographers pursuing stories but was not a functioning member of the news staff.

Although I was not a working observer, the observer effect (the idea that people may behave in an inconsistent or unnatural manner while being observed to please the observer) was alleviated by consistent presence (Adler & Adler, 1994). Though time did not permit me to become a completely naturalized part of the newsroom environment, conversation was easily engaged in and very natural, newsworkers were observed as quietly as possible, and newsworkers initiated conversations, often without prompting, that involved opinions about policy and other internal dynamics. Questions germane to this study were certainly asked as needed, and if elaboration was required, an interview was requested and scheduled for an off-duty time. Along with these tasks, I attended news meetings to observe policy-making and planning in process. Involvement in these day-to-day activities allowed access to newsworkers and management for observation and interviews. Staff members were asked to elaborate on daily decisions, as well as on organizational policy decisions in which they were directly or indirectly involved and that were indicative of or related to the phenomena observed in phase 1. This participant observation involved conducting more interviews, letting people tell their own stories as their unique culture was observed, and noting responses to situations as they occurred.

In each newsroom I was able to observe the rationale behind decision making and the interplay between newsworkers and managers. Such observation provided insight into institutional structure and the decision-making process. This was instrumental in discerning patterns across locations and the reasons the interaction and dynamics reported in this study occurred.

Documents

I was granted access to daily newsroom budgets, memos, and in a few cases, organizational research. In addition, individuals shared design handbooks, collective bargaining agreements (old and new), and historic documents about each of the publications. This constituted a valuable tool because it gave additional context to the observations I made and the policies being acted upon (or not acted upon) at each site. Pieced together and combined with other data, these documents allowed newsworkers to explain what this information meant to them in practical application and how they used this material in their jobs. The documents also presented another point of contrast between policy and reality.

Analysis of Field Notes

In the field, extensive jottings were taken at the newspaper sites in notebooks color coded for each publication. The *jottings*, lists of topics or events used in preparation for writing field notes (Emerson, Fretz, & Shaw, 1995), were explained as the notes were transcribed into dated and formal, categorized field notes. A binder of chronological observations was generated from these files. Initial analysis was done at every level of this process, noting recurring themes as they related to the interviews previously conducted and to the literature reviewed.

The data were then sorted and compared with findings in phase 1. This was an important step in that it served to separate the perceived realities of newsworkers from the ways these realities manifested in the newsrooms. Examples from field notes were taken to exemplify themes that were discovered. These data were classified according to the type of information they contained and were sorted into themes as examples of the observed or relayed events. Once the themes had been identified, they were collected into a narrative so the social realities could be more easily understood. As Emerson, Fretz, and Shaw (1995) explained:

> The ethnographer as author must represent the particular world he has studied (or some slice or quality of it) for readers who lack direct acquaintance with it. To do so, he moves back and forth between specific events recounted in field notes and more general concepts of interest to his discipline. An overconcern for scholarly framework and concepts would distort and obscure the nuances of everyday life; but to simply present members' categories exclusively in their terms would produce texts devoid of relevance and interest to scholarly audiences. (p. 169)

Appendix

The writing itself was another step in the analytic process. Laurel Richardson (1994) noted that the act of writing allows the researcher opportunities to further interpret findings as he or she makes those findings more accessible to an audience. Throughout the writing and analysis of this study, it was important to keep in mind that informants were influenced by their need to maintain their livelihoods and by the historical, cultural, and organizational nuances that existed between newspapers.

RATIONALE

The mixed qualitative method used in this study was selected for several reasons. To understand newsworker culture and the practices therein, I felt, one needed to be among those being studied. The work and reality of newsworkers were considered vital to an understanding of the way the profession operates in the contemporary world. The goal was to get as close to the action as possible while keeping the objectivity of an outsider for the sake of analysis. Inasmuch as this was a micro study, it is my hope that this work will add to a macro understanding of social constructionism in terms of the trends, routines, and influences already identified in the news industry by other researchers, and that the newsworker-oriented focus will add to a multifaceted literature base.

This study is by design exploratory. It certainly does not wholly adhere to ethnographic tradition, but elements of participant observation were vital for the integrity of the findings and for the human level of engagement desired in the study's conception. Incorporating interviews and informal conversations with people responsible for many different newspaper duties allowed a critical analysis of the challenged but important institution of newspaper journalism. The method was also appropriate for the theoretical traditions drawn upon for context.

Because this industry is changing, and no one can anticipate exactly what the future of newspapers will be, it was important to capture this period of uncertainty for posterity. The aim was a description and an understanding of the moment through the construction of the world of newsworkers. History will always determine the impact and lasting effect of subcultures—newsrooms included.

REFERENCES

Adler, P. A., & Adler, P. (1987). Observational techniques. In N. K. Denzin & Y. S. Lincoln (Eds.), *Handbook of qualitative research* (pp. 377–392). Thousand Oaks, CA: Sage.

Allen, S. (2006). *Online news: Journalist and the Internet.* Maidenhead, UK: Open University Press.

Aufderheide, P. (1999). *Communications policy and the public interest: The telecommunications act of 1996.* New York, NY: Guilford.

Bagdikian, B. H. (1990). *The media monopoly* (3rd ed.). Boston, MA: Beacon.

Becker, Vlad, Simpson, & Kalpen, 2012. *Annual survey of journalism and mass communication graduates.* Athens, GA: Association of Schools of Journalism and Mass Communication. Retrieved from http://www.grady.uga.edu/annualsurveys/Graduate_Survey/Graduate_2012/Grdrpt2012mergedv2.pdf

Berger, P. L., & Luckmann, T. (1966). *The social construction of reality: A treatise in the sociology of knowledge.* Garden City, NY: Doubleday.

Berkowitz, D. (1990). Refining the gatekeeping metaphor for local television news. *Journal of Broadcasting & Electronic Media, 34*(1), 55–68.

Berreman, G. D. (2007). Behind many masks: Ethnography and impression management. In A. C. G. M. Robben & J. A. Sluka (Eds.), *Ethnographic fieldwork: An anthropological reader* (pp. 137–158). Oxford, UK: Blackwell. (Original work published 1967).

Berte, K., & De Bens, E. (2008). Newspapers go for advertising. *Journalism Studies, 9*(5), 692–703.

Boczkowski, P. J. (2004). The mutual shaping of technology and society in Videotex newspapers: Beyond the diffusion and social shaping perspectives. *Information Society, 20*(4), 255–267.

Bourdieu, P. (1984). *Distinction: A social critique of the judgment of taste.* (Richard Nice, Trans.). New York, NY: Harvard University Press. (Original work published 1979).

Breed, W. (1955). Social control in the newsroom: A functional analysis. *Social Forces, 4,* 326–335.

Brennen, B. (2001). *For the record: An oral history of Rochester, New York.* New York, NY: Fordham University Press.

Bromley, M. (1997). The end of journalism? Changes in workplace practices in the press and broadcasting in the 1990s. In M. Bromley & T. O'Malley (Eds.), *A journalism reader* (pp. 330–350). London, UK: Routledge.

Cottle, S. (2003). Media organization and production: Mapping the field. In S. Cottle (Ed.), *Media organization and production* (pp. 3–6). London, UK: Sage.

de Botton, A. (2014). *The news: A user's manual.* London, UK: Penguin.

Deuze, M. (2007). *Media work.* Cambridge, UK: Polity.

Deuze, M. & Paulussen, S. (2002). Research note: Online journalism in the Low Countries; Basic, occupational and professional characteristics of online journalists in Flanders and the Netherlands. *European Journal of Communication, 17*(2), 237–245.

Domingo, D. (2008). Inventing online journalism: A constructivist approach to the development of online news. In C. A. Patterson & D. Domingo (Eds.), *Making online news: The Ethnography of New Media Production* (pp. 15–28). New York, NY: Peter Lang.

Domingo, D., Quandt, T., Heinonen, A., Paulssen, S., Singer, J. B., & Vujnovic, M. (2008). Participatory journalism practices in the media and beyond: An international comparative study of initiatives in online newspapers. *Journalism Practice, 2*(3), 326–342.

Durkheim, E. (2008). *The elementary forms of religious life.* (C. Cosman, Trans.). New York, NY: Oxford University Press. (Original work published 1912).

Eadies, W. F. (2009). *21st century communication: A reference handbook.* Thousand Oaks, CA: Sage.

References

Emerson, R. M., Fretz, R. I., & Shaw, L. L. (1995). *Writing ethnographic fieldnotes*. Chicago, IL: University of Chicago Press.

Entman, R. M. (1991). Framing U.S. coverage of international news: Contrasts in narratives of the KAL and Iran Air incidents. *Journal of Communication, 41*(4), 6–27.

Epstein, E. J. (1973). *News from nowhere: Television and the news*. New York, NY: Random House.

Foucault, M. (1970). *The order of things: An archaeology of human science*. New York, NY: Random House. (Original work published as *Les mots et les choses* in 1966).

Gamson, W. A., Croteau, D., Hoynes, W., & Sasson T. (1992). Media images and the social construction of reality. *Annual Review of Sociology, 18*, 373–393.

Gans, H. (2004). *Deciding what is news: A study of CBS Evening News, NBC Nightly News, Newsweek and Time*. Evanston, IL: Northwestern University Press. (Original work published 1979).

Garrison, B. (2001). Diffusion of online information technologies in newspaper newsrooms. *Journalism, 2*(2), 221–239.

Giddens, A. (1984). *The constitution of society*. Cambridge, UK: Polity.

Gitlin, T. (1980). *The whole world is watching: Mass media in the making and unmaking of the New Left*. Berkeley, CA: University of California Press.

Glasgow University Media Group. (1976). *Bad news*. London, UK: Routledge & Kegan Paul.

Glasgow University Media Group. (1980). *More bad news*. Boston, MA: Routledge & Kegan Paul.

Goffman, E. (1974). *Frame analysis*. New York, NY: Harper Colophon.

Golding, P., & Murdock G. (1999). Culture, communications, and political economy. In H. Tumber (Ed.), *News: A reader* (pp. 155–165). New York, NY: Oxford University Press.

Gramsci, A. (2000). *The Antonio Gramsci reader: Selected writings.* (D. Forgacs, Ed.). New York, NY: Random House. (Original work published 1840).

Greenwald, M., & Bernt, J. (2000). *The big chill: Investigative reporting in the current media environment.* Ames, IA: Iowa State University Press.

Hall, S. (1999). *Representations and the media.* Northampton, NH: Media Education Foundation.

Hallin, D. C. (1985). The American news media: A critical theory perspective. In J. Forester (Ed.), *Critical theory and public life* (pp. 121–146). Cambridge, MA: MIT Press.

Hardt, H. (1990). Newsworkers: Technology and journalism history. *Critical studies in mass communication, 7,* 346–365.

Hardt, H., & Brennen, B. (1995). Introduction. In H. Hardt & B. Brennen (Eds.), *Newsworkers: Toward a history of the rank and file* (pp. vii–xii). Minneapolis, MN: University of Minnesota Press.

Heider, D. (2000). *White news: Why local news programs don't cover people of color.* Mahwah, NJ: Lawrence Erlbaum.

Herman, E. S., & Chomsky, N. (1988). *Putting reality together: BBC news.* Beverly Hills, CA: Sage.

Hirsch, P. (2000). Cultural industries revisited. *Organizational Science, 11*(3), 356–361.

Johnson-Cartee, K. S. (2005). *News narratives and news framing.* Oxford, UK: Rowman & Littlefield.

Karp, S. (2007, July 17). Newspaper online vs. print ad revenue: The 10% problem. *Publishing 2.0.* Retrieved from http://publishing2.com/2007/07/17/newspaper-online-vs-print-ad-revenue-the-10-problem/

Klinenberg, E. (2005). Convergence: News production in a digital age. *Annals of the American Academy of Political and Social Science, 597,* 48–64.

Kopper, C. G., Kolthoff, A., & Czepek, A. (2000). Research review: Online journalism—A report on current and continuing research and major questions in the international discussion. *Journalism Studies, 1,* 499–512.

Leedy, P. D., & Ormond J. E. (2001). *Practical research: Planning and design.* Upper Saddle River, NJ: Merrill Prentice Hall.

Marx, K., & Engels F. (1998). *The communist manifesto.* London, UK: Penguin Books. Signet Classic. (Original work published 1848).

Mayer, M. (1987). *Making news.* Garden City, NY: Doubleday.

Mitchelstein, E., & Boczkowski, P. J. (2009). Between tradition and change: A review of recent research on online news production. *Journalism, 10*(5), 562–586.

Molotch, H., & Lester, M. (1974). News as purposive behavior: On the strategic use of routine events, accidents, and scandals. *American Sociological Review, 39*, 101–112.

Murdock, G. (1973). Political deviance: The press presentation of a militant mass demonstration. In S. Cohen & J. Young (Eds.). *The manufacture of news: A reader* (pp. 853–872). Beverly Hills, CA: Sage.

Nerone, J., & Barnhurst, K. G. (2001). Beyond modernism: Digital design, Americanization and the future of newspaper form. *New Media & Society, 3*(4), 467–482.

Newspaper Guild, Communication Workers of America. (2012). The guild's mission. Retrieved from http://www.newsguild.org/about

Pew Research Center for People and the Press. (2004). *How journalists see journalists.* Washington, DC: Pew Research Center for People and the Press.

Pew Research Center for People and the Press. (2008). *State of the news media.* Washington, DC: Pew Research Center for People and the Press. Retrieved May 1, 2014, from http://stateofthenewsmedia.com/2008/index.asp

Pew Research Center for People and the Press. (2014). *State of the news media 2014: Overview.* Washington, DC: Pew Research Center for People and the Press. Retrieved May 7, 2014, from http://www.journalism.org/packages/state-of-the-news-media-2014/

Richardson, L. (1994). A method of inquiry. In N. K. Denzin & Y. S. Lincoln (Eds.), *Handbook of Qualitative Research* (pp. 516–529). Thousand Oaks, CA: Sage.

Robben, A. C. G. M., & Sluka J. A. (2007). Fieldwork in cultural anthropology: An introduction. In A. C. G. M. Robben & J. Sluka (Eds.), *Ethnographic fieldwork: An anthropological reader* (pp. 1–39). Oxford, UK: Blackwell.

Rothenbuhler, E. W. (1998). *Ritual communication: From everyday conversation to mediated ceremony.* Thousand Oaks, CA: Sage.

Schlesinger, P. (1978). *Putting "reality" together: BBC news.* London, UK: Constable.

Schlesinger, P. (1999). From production to propaganda. In P. Scannell & P. Schlesinger (Eds.), *Culture and power* (pp. 283–306). London, UK: Sage.

Shepard, A. C. (1996). Consultants in the newsroom. *American Journalism Review, 18*(7), 19.

Shoemaker, P. J. (1999). Gatekeeping. In H. Tumber (Ed.), *News: A reader* (pp. 73–78). New York, NY: Oxford University Press.

Shoemaker, P. J., & Reese, S. D. (1996). *Mediating the message: Theories of influence on mass media content* (2nd ed.). New York, NY: Longman.

Singer, J. B. (2003). Who are these guys? The online challenge to the notion of journalistic professionalism. *Journalism, 4*(2), 139–163.

Siu, W. (2009). Social Construction of Reality: The Tobacco Issue. *Critical Public Health, 19*(1), 23–44.

Smith, E. (n.d.) Totals. In *Paper cuts.* Retrieved from http://newspaperlayoffs.com

Stucke, M. E., & Grunes A. P. (2009). Toward a better competition policy for the media: The challenge of developing antitrust policies that support the media sector's unique role in our democracy. *Connecticut Law Review, 7*(101), 103–146.

Teamsters. (n.d.). Newspaper, magazine and electronic media workers. *Teamsters: North America's Strongest Union.* Retrieved from http://teamster.org/content/newspaper-magazine-and-electronic-media-workers

References

Tourish, D., Paulsen, N., Hobman, E., & Bordia, P. (2004). The downsides of downsizing. *Management Communication Quarterly, 17*(4), 485–516.

Tuchman, G. (1972). Objectivity as strategic Ritual: An examination of newsmen's notions of objectivity. *American Journal of Sociology, 77*(4), 660–679.

Tuchman, G. (1976). What is news? Telling stories. *Journal of Communication, 26*(4), 93–97.

Tuchman, G. (1978). *Making news: A study in the construction of reality.* New York, NY: Free Press.

Turow, J. (1997). *Breaking up America: Advertising and the new media world.* Chicago, IL: University of Chicago Press.

Underwood, D. (1993). *When MBAs rule the newsroom: How marketers and managers are reshaping today's media.* New York, NY: Columbia University Press.

White, D. M. (1950). The 'gatekeeper': A case study in the selection of news. *Journalism Quarterly, 27*, 383–390.

World Editors Forum, Reuters, Zogby International. (2008). Integrated newsroom will be the norm. Retrieved from http://www.livemint.com/r/LiveMint/Period1/oldpdf/a15b8fc0-21fd-4c96-ba0d-58478688f26d.pdf

Yang, N. (2013). A fresh perspective: How consultants are reenergizing newsrooms and ad sales. *Editor & Publisher.* Retrieved from http://www.editorandpublisher.com/Features/Article/A-Fresh-Perspective--How-Consultants-Are-Reenergizing-Newsrooms-and-Ad-Sales

Index

ambition, 57
autonomy, 20–21, 27, 29, 32, 45, 58, 65, 94, 101–104, 116, 122, 124, 129, 132

Bagdikian, Ben, 15, 64
Berreman, Gerald, 27
"Behind Many Masks," 27
Berkowitz, Daniel, 21
Berger, Peter, 4, 12–13, 22
Bernt, Joseph, 24–25
big-picture decisions, 107, 117
black ceiling, 8, 98, 114–115, 117, 124, 132
Boczkowski, Pablo J., 11–12, 19, 22
Bourdieu, Pierre, 17, 127
breaking news, 38, 41–42, 89–90, 93, 98, 102
Brennen, Bonnie, 2, 5, 20, 22–23, 70
Breed, Warren, 6–7, 14, 29, 38, 46, 67–68, 70, 72, 77, 80–82, 94, 102, 106
budgets, 28–29, 39, 93, 136, 141

Chomsky, Noam, 16–17
civic duty, 7, 54, 86, 108, 119
civic function, 3, 6, 29, 36, 68, 121, 126, 132
controlling behavior, 29
Cottle, Simon, 30

de Botton, Alain, 11, 26
design centers, 42
Deuze, Mark, 19, 22
digital specialists, 4, 6, 38, 76, 110,

digital specialists (*continued*), 127
Durkheim, Émile, 16, 20, 22, 121, 123

Elementary Forms of Religious Life, The, 20
Epstein, Edward Jay, 18, 111
Entman, Robert, 26

Foucault, Michel, 19
Fourth Estate, 5, 120, 122
furloughs, 84

Gannett, Frank, 23, 44
Gans, Herbert, 27–29
Giddens, Anthony, 25
Gitlin, Todd, 25
Glasgow University Media Group, 18
Goffman, Erving, 25
Gramsci, Antonio, 23, 125
Greenwald, Marilyn, 24–25

Hall, Stuart, 25
Hardt, Hanno, 2, 5, 20, 29, 121
hegemony, 17, 23–24, 129
Herman, Edward, 16–17
human capital, 3

in-groupness, 81
Internet, 2, 9, 12, 25, 28–29, 38, 56, 90, 116
inventory, 42

Klinenberg, Eric, 12

layoffs, 7–8, 27, 43, 47, 49, 56, 60, 72, 78, 80–82, 84–87, 93–94, 104, 107–108, 114, 121, 126–127, 129
legacy, 54–55
Lester, Marilyn, 24, 65
loyalty, 9, 77, 85, 108, 117
Luckmann, Thomas, 4, 12–13, 22

manna, 22, 121, 123
Marx, Karl, 16–17, 120
mechanical solidarity, 16–17
Mitchelstein, Eugenia, 11–12
mobility, 11, 29, 46, 72–73, 75, 89
Molotch, Harvey, 24, 65
Murdock, Graham, 22

news gatherers, 6, 14, 24, 41, 52, 55
news judgment, 115, 125
newsworkers, 1–9, 11–14, 16–18, 20–22, 24–27, 29–32, 35–37, 40–46, 49–54, 56–60, 63–65, 67–68, 70–78, 80–88, 91–92, 94–95, 97–99, 101–117, 119–132, 135–144

operational directives, 30, 37, 39, 43–46, 52, 103, 112, 124

photography, 7, 43, 45, 53, 65, 71, 79–80, 98, 112, 123, 128, 138
presenters, 6, 41, 47, 87, 93, 95
products, 23, 29–30, 42–43, 51, 54, 71, 75, 77, 79, 110–112, 121, 123, 126, 132

Reese, Stephen, 13, 15, 63–64, 66, 124
regrets, 52
reporters, 1, 4, 14, 30, 37–40, 43–44, 47, 50, 52–53, 68, 71–72, 75,

reporters (*continued*), 87–89, 93, 102–103, 107, 110, 113, 128, 136, 140
resistance, 8, 14, 101–102, 104, 106–107, 109, 116, 125
ritual, 14, 19–21, 32, 119–120, 123–124
Rothenbuhler, Eric, 21, 32, 120, 122–123

Schlesinger, Philip, 15–16, 45, 124, 128
Shoemaker, Pamela, 13–15, 63–64, 66, 124
Siu, Wanda, 19
Sluka, Jeffrey, 27
social capital, 17, 127
social construction, 4, 12, 14, 25, 31–32, 135, 143
social control, 5, 14–15, 20, 29, 67, 83, 91, 94, 119
social distance, 94
social fact, 16
soft skills, 127
sunshine blogs, 8, 114–115, 117

Telecommunications Act of 1996, 28
technology, 5–8, 22, 24, 27, 29, 36–37, 43–44, 64, 71–72, 76, 88–90, 109, 120–121, 128
time management, 79, 87, 92
traditional tasks, 64, 98, 117, 119, 122, 127–128
Turow, Joseph, 19
Tuchman, Gaye, 11, 14, 25, 91

Underwood, Doug, 17–18, 30, 43, 94–95, 124
United Way, The, 105–106

watchdog, 24, 36, 51, 54, 97, 119, 123

When MBAs Rule the Newsroom, 17
White, David Manning, 14, 21, 140

www.ingramcontent.com/pod-product-compliance
Lightning Source LLC
Chambersburg PA
CBHW022012160426
43197CB00007B/393